CIRCLE PLAY

Simple Designs for Fabulous Fabrics

Reynola Pakusich

C&T PUBLISHING

PUBLISHER: *Amy Marson*

EDITORIAL DIRECTOR: *Gailen Runge*

EDITOR: *Cyndy Lyle Rymer*

TECHNICAL EDITOR: *Gael Betts*

COPYEDITOR/PROOFREADER: *Gael Betts, Stacy Chamness, Susan Nelson*

COVER DESIGNER: *Kristen Yenche*

DESIGN DIRECTOR/BOOK DESIGNER: *Rose Sheifer*

ILLUSTRATOR: *Jeffery Carrillo*

PRODUCTION ASSISTANT: *Matthew Allen*

PHOTOGRAPHY: *Sharon Risedorph, Luke Mulks*

Published by C&T Publishing, Inc., P.O. Box 1456, Lafayette, California 94549

Front cover: *Circles 1*
Back cover: Detail from *Cosmic Ribbons* page 59, *Plaid Circles I* page 54

Attention Teachers: C&T Publishing, Inc. encourages you to use this book as a text for teaching. Contact us at 800-284-1114 or www.ctpub.com for more information about the C&T Teachers Program.

Library of Congress Cataloging-in-Publication Data
Pakusich, Barbara Reynola.
  Circle play simple designs for fabulous fabrics / Barbara Reynola Pakusich.
    p. cm.
  Includes bibliographical references and index.
  ISBN 1-57120-235-8
  1. Quilting. 2. Patchwork. I. Title.
TT835.P33 2004   746.46—dc22
2004001397
Printed in China
10 9 8 7 6 5 4 3 2 1

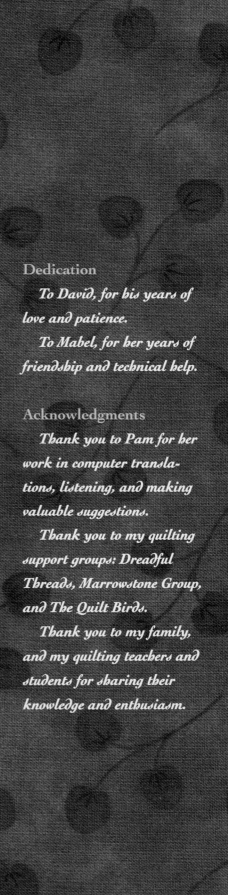

Dedication
To David, for his years of love and patience.
To Mabel, for her years of friendship and technical help.

Acknowledgments
Thank you to Pam for her work in computer translations, listening, and making valuable suggestions.
Thank you to my quilting support groups: Dreadful Threads, Marrowstone Group, and The Quilt Birds.
Thank you to my family, and my quilting teachers and students for sharing their knowledge and enthusiasm.

Contents

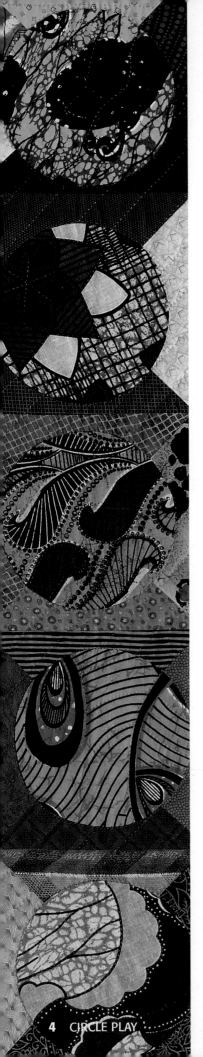

Preface

Circle Play is a process that focuses on how to use the beautiful fabrics you have collected but, like many quilters, may be hesitant to cut into. Read through the entire book, which is organized in the same order you would make a quilt, and then go back and start the *Circle Play* process.

Explore fabric selection. The wonderful theme fabrics that are used, enhanced, and incorporated into the quilt along with an ample collection of support fabrics. The generous quantity of fabrics is intended to reflect the collecting process of many quilters. The *Circle Play* process lends itself to making a series of quilts, so a large variety of support fabrics is highlighted. The fabrics used (or fabrics that you were unable to use) in a Circle Play I (beginning *Circle Play*) quilt can happily find homes in subsequent Circle Play II and III quilts. Diana Johnston created a series of five quilts. See pages 70–71.

Chapter 1 discusses fabric selection for the circles and background blocks, including the characteristics of value and texture, as well as nontraditional fabrics. Blocks from a teaching sample help to explore the concepts of *Circle Play* quilts.

You are encouraged to look at quilt design and fabric in an entirely new way.

Chapters 2 and 3 cover the process of selecting and constructing the circles and blocks. You are encouraged to look at quilt design and fabric in an entirely new way. Also, the concept of fabric design-line flow (see Glossary, page 76) is introduced. A teaching sample provides further ways to develop your Circle Play quilt.

Chapter 4 explains circle and block composition, using examples from three teaching samples. In Teaching Sample 1 circles and backgrounds are designed unit by unit. Teaching Sample 2 focuses on developing the quilt background before the circles are added. This model uses only two fabrics for the entire quilt top, offering stress relief from the fabric collecting of Chapter 1. Teaching Sample 3 arranges a collection of circles before designing the background pieces into blocks.

Chapter 5 introduces another teaching sample used to demonstrate a variety of border techniques. A close look at the borders in the Gallery quilts offers additional inspiration.

Chapter 6 offers an assortment of ideas for backing, quilting, and a variety of binding techniques to enhance your quilt.

Chapter 7 further develops the *Circle Play* concept. Second and third generation quilts develop from the previous quilt and use the same fabrics, along with pieces you couldn't resist buying while making the first quilt. We'll explore some of the previous design options, and satisfy some of the "what ifs" that will continue to fuel your fascination with *Circle Play* as they do mine.

A Circle Play Primer

Many of the beautiful fabrics we collect seem to fit more "comfortably" in a circular shape than in the more traditional straight lines of squares and triangles. As shown in the photo below, the circles and their backgrounds can be used to create a diagonal value flow of light that can turn or move with subtlety or drama.

Background blocks are pieced from two, three, or four triangles, and are used to create the value flow of light *behind* the circles. You will learn how to use the blocks and the triangles that form the background to integrate the textural lines, colors, and values of the circles in the foreground.

Begin your journey by exploring the integration and relationship between the circle and its supporting player, the background block. Here are some of the techniques for designing with circles.

Relate the values and colors of the circles to the triangular divisions of the background block; this obscures the individual shapes.

Combine the design line (see Glossary, page 76) of the circle with the design line of a triangle to continue the flow of the design line.

Extend the design line from a circle to its background triangle and beyond to an adjacent background triangle and its circle.

I hope you enjoy your exploration into *Circle Play* quilts!

VERT COTERIE, 40" x 40", by Reynola Pakusich. The value flow of this quilt creates an unusual X design that is emphasized by using two second-generation circles.

Selecting Fabrics

When designing a *Circle Play* quilt, you can assemble a collection of fabrics or choose one wonderful piece of fabric for all the circles. When selecting a single fabric, look for designs that have the following characteristics.

Scale, Density, Shape, Texture, and Value

1. Scale: small to large motifs.
2. Density: less space vs. more space between motifs.
3. Shape: flowing curves vs. geometric lines.
4. Texture: interesting backgrounds behind the motifs.
5. Value: how light or dark a fabric reads.

Fabrics for circles

Here are examples of fabrics that have all, or at least several, of the fabric selection characteristics. Fabrics 1 and 2 feature the greatest variety of line, sizes, and shapes, including background texture. Fabric 3 has less variety of shape and texture but a greater degree of value contrast. Fabrics 4 and 5 have good line variety and more color variation. Fabric 6 has good density and color variety even with a solid orange background.

Fabric for Circles: One Fabric or More?

CIRCLES FROM A SINGLE FABRIC

If you begin with only a half yard and decide to expand the quilt size, consider additional fabrics with similar color and character. The photo below shows the original theme fabric with two companion fabrics. The two additional fabrics are similar Japanese prints but differ a bit in color, density, and value from the original.

Tip

A half yard of a single fabric with similar textures would make enough circles for a nine-block quilt; a yard could be stretched to make sixteen to twenty-five blocks.

Theme fabric with two companions

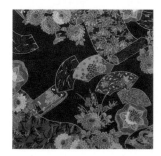

Detail from **WHY NOT BLACK AND WHITE?** page 78

CIRCLES FROM A VARIETY OF FABRICS

When selecting a variety of fabrics for the circles, start with a theme. This might be texture, such as plaids, or a collection of black-and-white prints.

Fabric selection can also begin with a subject or color theme, such as ethnic fabrics with leaves, as shown in the quilts on page 8.

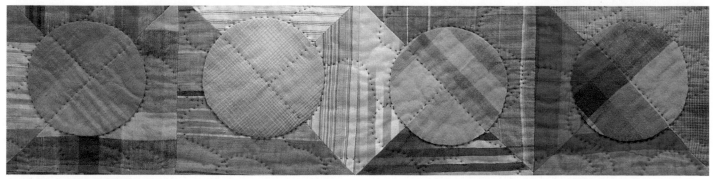

Detail from **PLAID CIRCLES** page 54

AFRICAN CIRCLES I, 45" x 45", by Reynola Pakusich

Yukata Swallows is a beautiful combination of teal, blue, and yellow; *Japanese Ladies* relies on red and black prints; and a collection of African-print sample swatches is featured in *African Circles I.*

NONTRADITIONAL FABRIC

Some quilters have collections of smaller scraps of beautiful fabrics that are not the traditional quilter's 100% cotton. The *Circle Play* technique is a wonderful option because it allows control and stabilization of slippery or loosely woven fabrics during construction. In these examples, I used color as a limiting factor, the blue and brown of *Japanese Circles I* (page 31) in which most circles are made from vintage kimono wools, and *Asilomar Circles I* (page 63), which features vintage Japanese silks and wools in brown and red.

Focus on color first and limit the project to three to four colors when you use a wide variety of fabrics in a collection, such as an African group. African fabrics are very graphic and dramatic, and it will be easy to recognize the five guidelines of fabric selection—scale, density, shape, texture, and value—within those color limitations.

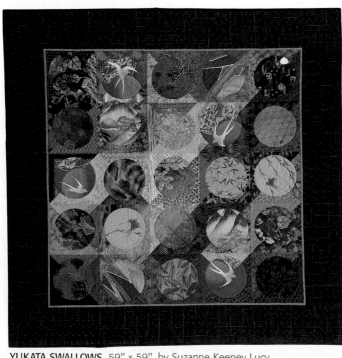

YUKATA SWALLOWS, 59" x 59", by Suzanne Keeney Lucy

JAPANESE LADIES, 46" x 47", by Annette Anderson

Background Fabrics

Study your theme fabric or circle-fabric collection for color identity when selecting fabrics for the background blocks. Stretch each of the identified colors or hues to both sides of itself on the color wheel. If you choose to use green, for example, include teal (blue-green) and lime (yellow-green). The color stretch might be individual tone-on-tone fabrics or a print that includes both teal and lime. The theme fabrics usually provide clues for these color stretches.

COLOR QUANTITY

For support fabrics, repeat the color quantities as in the theme fabric. For example, the support fabrics for this theme fabric include mostly browns, reds, and golds that reflect the orange and golds of the theme, many greens, and a few purples. When I buy support fabrics, I usually purchase one-third to half yard amounts. If I am trading with a friend, I keep a fat quarter.

VALUE CHANGE

Stretch the values of each color used to include the full range of light to dark for each color. Study the theme fabric for the degree of value change within the fabric. The degree of value change in the support fabric should be similar to, or less than, the degree of value change in the theme fabric. You don't want the support fabrics to overwhelm or distract from the theme fabric. Visual texture needs to be considered in the colors and values selected.

The Group A textures below are drawn from the support fabrics for Teaching Sample l. They are mostly tone-on-tones that will be used to create and smooth the value flow of the background. They will help disguise the design lines of the circles with the seamlines of the blocks. Many read as solid prints, but on closer

YUKATA SWALLOWS II, 50" x 50", by Suzanne Keeney Lucy

Teaching Sample 1:
Theme fabric

Tip

Keep the degree of value contrast the same as or less than the theme fabric while stretching the variety of texture.

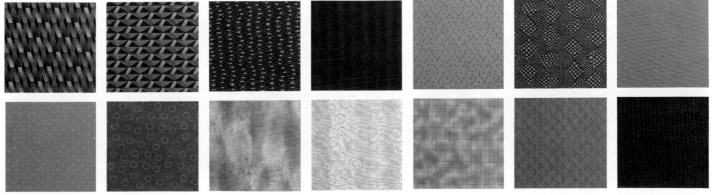

Group A textures for value flow

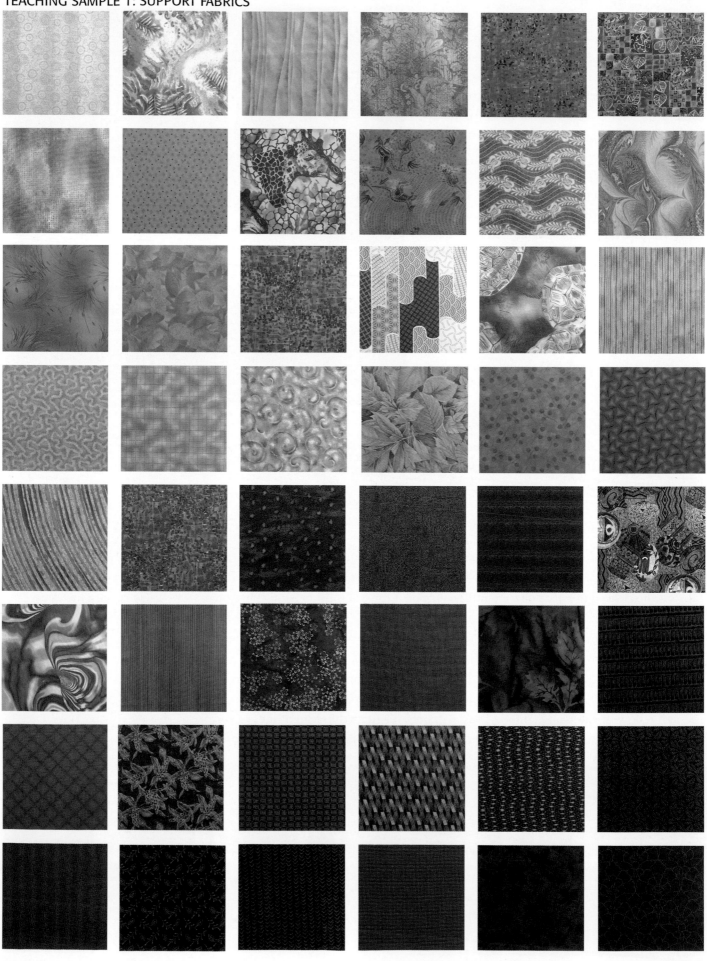

inspection will show a great deal of variety in sizes, shapes, and lines (curved and straight, painterly or defined). Ombré (shaded) fabrics are very useful.

Group B textures, also drawn from the support fabrics, will carry the design lines of the circles to the design lines within the triangles of the pieced background blocks. The colors and values of the circle fabrics are represented here, but the textures will be larger and more defined. In the photos below, note that most fabrics are still tone-on-tone but have flowing lines and fall within the degree of value change of the theme fabric(s).

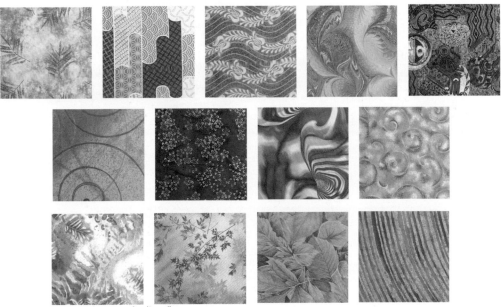

Group B textures for line flow

Consider fabrics for either value or line flow with wonderful texture but which may have an unexpected shape or image: giraffe heads, mountains, tigers, and bamboo. Methods for handling these fabrics are covered in Chapters 2 and 3.

Group C textures with value and line flow that are more important than the shapes

Include special pieces of wool, silk, or blends from your fabric stash. Choose a broad selection of support fabrics for color and value. Support fabric textures are chosen for general interest and, more importantly, to blend the textural lines of the circles with the textural and seamlines of the backgrounds.

Just the Beginning

The following blocks from Teaching Sample 1 (Chapter 4, page 27) demonstrate the excitement of circles and background integration that forms the heart of this book.

The brown tone-on-tone triangle construction line is used to disguise the dark triangle shape within the circle.

Here is a detail of the textural movement between blocks that moves the design line from the white flower in the circle of the left block to the orange line across the seamline and on to the next circle.

Notice how the two different green swirls cause the design to flow between the two blocks.

In this block the green textured fabric integrates the construction-line triangular shape with the design in the circle.

This is just the beginning of *Circle Play*.

New fabrics may always be added for backgrounds or circles. The relationship between the circles and the blocks can be as detailed as you choose; quilts in Gallery I (page 13) represent many degrees of complexity.

While working on *Circle Play* quilts I have noticed two things: I keep buying fabric for the quilt (sometimes even after the quilt is finished!), and there are not enough places in the project to use all the fabulous fabrics I selected for that quilt!

CIRCLES I, 60" x 60",
by Reynola Pakusich

UNTAMED, 32"x 24",
by Joanne Corfield.
This quilt includes all the
design features of the
Circle Play concept in just
six blocks! The background
textures repeat the circle
textures while changing
size and density. The
binding choice nicely
finishes the quilt design.

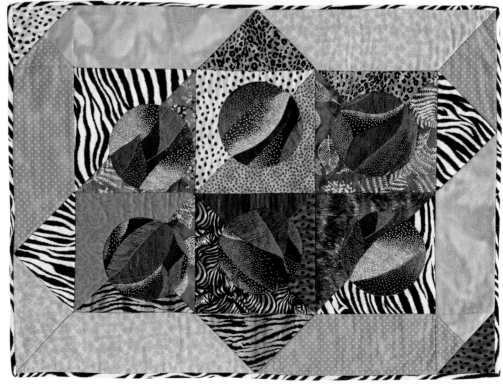

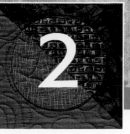
Using a variety of fabrics for circles enables you to showcase more fabrics. Include quiet as well as dramatic favorites within your selected color range. For artistic repetition and visual flow across the finished quilt include two circles from each fabric. Often the pairs of circles have such design variety it becomes a challenge to locate the pairs!

NEVER-ENDING CIRCLES II, 59" x 59", by Mabel Huseby. This second-generation quilt is calmer and seems to have a stronger value flow.

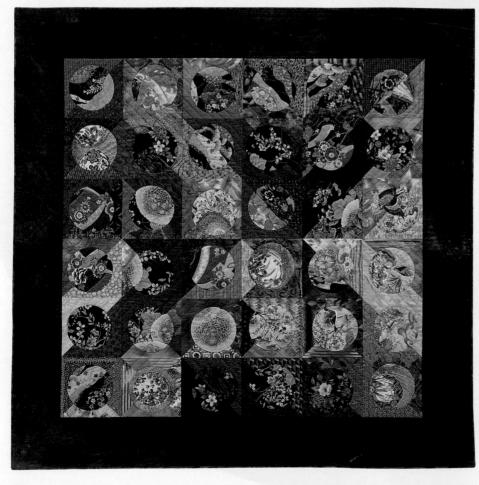

NEVER-ENDING CIRCLES I, 68" x 68", by Mabel Huseby. The variety of fabrics used for the circles, the skill used in relating the circles to background, and the value-flow inspire the viewer to "never be finished looking at it."

If you choose a single wonderful fabric for the circles you can reduce the number of design decisions to be made by half. You can also end up with a great quilt if most of the decisions are confined to the background fabrics only. We will continue to use the theme fabrics selected in Chapter 1 and Teaching Sample 1 on page 27 to demonstrate circle selection and design options.

Theme fabric

Auditioning Circle Sizes

After selecting your fabric the next decision is the size of the circle you want to use. Use plates, cups, and bowls as a quick reference for circle size and to trace around to make templates. I mark the diameter measurements on the template, and on the bottom of each dish, in case I need to make a new template.

AUDITIONING CIRCLES

Make circle windows (one size per page) from newsprint or other plain paper in at least three different sizes. Use these windows to select the circle size most suited to the theme fabric by gliding the circle window across the fabric. The photographs show circle windows in various sizes on the same fabric. Note that the smallest circle makes the design feel "cramped." The largest circle shows even more variety of density and line flow than the middle size.

Teaching Sample 1 uses the medium window, a 5¼" circle.

Glide the different circle templates across the fabric to select the circle size that is most appealing.

Base the size of the circle on the amount of fabric you have. You can cut nine circles from a half to one yard of fabric, or cut six to ten circles from a favorite collection. **Check that the largest circle window will fit on the collection pieces.** Keep the size and use of the finished quilt in mind: Will it be a nine-block wall-hanging or a bed-size quilt? A large, bed-size quilt made with larger circles will need fewer blocks than if you use smaller circles and blocks.

Tip

A half yard of fabric will usually make at least nine circles. Chapter 4, Composing Circle Quilts, discusses what you can do if you need one or two circles more than the theme fabric provides. (Don't panic!)

Tip

I trace around my dishes to make the template patterns.

Making freezer-paper circles the quick way

A single circle window, with seamlines indicated, to help with circle selection and placement

FINALIZE YOUR CIRCLES

After you have selected the size of your circle, cut a single circle window from newsprint; use the window to fine-tune circle placement. Place marks at the four quarter-circle points on the circle window to indicate the possible seamlines of the background blocks. Use this circle window to make freezer-paper templates for each circle to be used in the quilt.

Try to visualize the design portion of the circle fabric meeting with the fabric and seamlines of the background blocks. These meeting points make a combination of up to four triangle fabrics and four seamlines. In the example below, the fabric in the window is made up of one dark quarter, three quarters that have busy design lines, several colors, and a dense texture. The curving ribbons within the dark quarter could be used to meet with the seamline and flow onto the quarter-triangle of the background block. Continue using this window to select the remaining circles you'll need.

The examples below demonstrate two important design considerations:
1. Design lines from the circle fabrics can be used to continue the seamlines of the background block.
2. The design lines of the circle can align with the design lines of the background triangles.

This second design concept is subtle in the finished quilt and serves as a wonderful personal challenge for the quiltmaker. It can be a wonderful discovery for the viewer, too, and is most effective when it happens a few times in the entire quilt. It wouldn't be much of a discovery if it happened in each block!

Design lines align with the seamlines.

Design lines flow and merge with the background design lines.

CIRCLE CHOICES

When you are pleased with the circle framed within the circle window, pin a freezer-paper circle, shiny side down, through the window onto the right side of the fabric and move on to select the next circle. Leave a generous ½" allowance around each circle (and at least 1" between circles). Peek under the outside edge of the window to check the seam allowance, especially at the edge of the fabric.

Grainline is not an issue with circles; the focus is on what happens within the circle. Avoid centering any object within the circle; this prevents the integration of the circle design with its background block. Also, body "parts" are more interesting than the whole. Part of an eye, tail, foot, or leaf provides mystery and encourages the viewer to look further and use their imagination to complete the image.

Cutting the Circles

Place the fabric with the selected circles flat on the ironing board. Remove the pins and press with a dry iron to bond the freezer paper to the fabric. Rough cut around each circle, leaving a generous ½" seam allowance. Peel the freezer paper off the right side of the fabric, and center it (shiny side down) on the *wrong* side of the circle fabric; iron it to the fabric. Leave the freezer-paper circles in place until we get to page 38 in Chapter 4. The freezer-paper circles can be used several times for future projects. Place the circles on your design wall to prevent exact duplicates. The viewer will enjoy the slight differences.

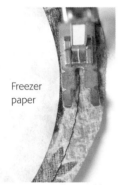

Freezer paper

Sew a presser-foot width from the edge of the paper.

PREPARING TO SEW

Set the sewing machine for a gathering stitch, about six stitches to the inch. With the freezer paper side up, sew ¼" from the outside edge of the paper circle (approximately the width of the presser foot) or midway between the paper circle and the edge of the fabric if the seam allowance is slightly less than ½".

Stop sewing before you reach the first stitch, and do not backstitch. Leave the thread tails long as you remove the circle from the machine. Secure the beginning and ending threads on the right side of the fabric (the bobbin threads). Carefully gather the fabric along the thread, one side at a time, until the fabric circle gathers into a cup around the freezer paper with the wrong side of the fabric inside the cup.

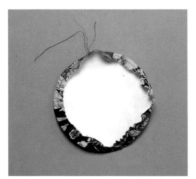

Gather the circle into a cup.

When the cup is formed, turn the circle over and press the seam allowance smooth at the edge of the freezer paper. Ease any tightness as you press. Gathering first and releasing as needed forms a smoother line. To prevent the gathers from loosening, place the long threads at the two ends of the stitching under the freezer paper and press to hold. Continue pressing the circle curve. With a little practice this will form a smooth circle that is ready to audition for its background block in Chapter 3.

The background blocks are made of half-square and quarter-square triangles. You can use the triangles in several ways.

- Create a quiet background so the circles are the main focus.
- Blend the triangles with the circles, so portions of the circles fade into the background.
- Continue the beautiful design lines of the circles onto the design lines of the background triangle fabrics.
- Form light and dark swaths of value flow across the quilt and behind the circles.

There are five steps for designing the background blocks:

1. Decide the finished size of the background block; see page 19 for guidelines.
2. Consider the design components of value, color, and line placement.
3. Determine the number of triangles to use for each block: two, three, or four.
4. Decide how you will make the triangles; use the special rotary rulers to cut the triangles, or make your own plastic templates.
5. Cut and construct the block.

FROGGIES, 24" x 24", by Cheryl Gillman. The frog fabric used in all of the circles is backlit beautifully by the warm values, while the strong dark greens create a dramatic contrast.

Size of the Block

Cut square window templates in three sizes to audition background blocks for the circles you constructed in Chapter 2.

In the photographs that follow, notice the amount of space between the circle and the sides of the square.

In the first photo, a 7" finished block seems a bit tight or close. The second photo features a 9" finished block; the circle seems lost in the added space rather than being the focus. The third photograph, an 8" finished block, is just right. The 8" block allows room to adjust the circle to the construction and design lines, without overwhelming the circle.

Tip

Like Goldilocks and the Three Bears, try three sizes to decide which is the best background size for the circles; the background will be 2"–4" larger than the circle.

7" block, too small

9" block, too large

8" block, just right

Triangles and Other Design Components

Use the chosen size of square window template to audition each circle with various fabrics; look for color, value, and design lines. Place the background fabric behind the window to give you an idea of what the block would look like. Each background block should enhance the corresponding circle. Teaching Sample 2 in Chapter 4 relates the background blocks to each other before combining the circles with the blocks. For now, we'll attempt to marry the background to the circle first. The background triangles for each circle are individually cut, reducing the number of leftover triangles at the completion of the quilt top.

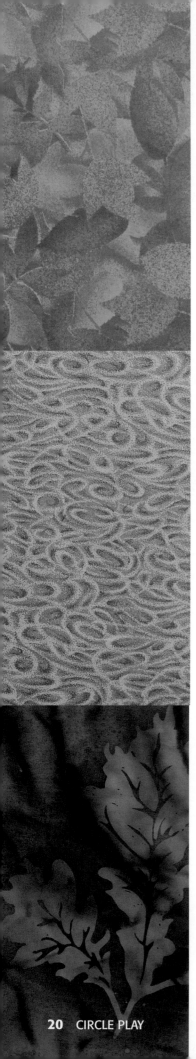

VALUE FLOW ACROSS THE BACKGROUND

For the smoothest value flow across the entire background, plan to make most of the blocks with two half-square triangles, fewer blocks with three triangles (one half-square triangle and two quarter-square triangles), and only a few blocks with four quarter-square triangles.

The photos that follow show the same circle auditioned with various background blocks. The seamline of the dark triangle is disguised as your eye follows the line of the circle. Block 1, with only two triangles, has a quiet, calm texture that shows off the circle while repeating its color and value. This is important for creating quiet areas of the quilt. Block 2, where the lighter half-square triangle is divided into two quarter-square triangles, adds interest by repeating the "busy-ness" of the circle's texture, and results in blending or softening that edge of the circle.

Block 1: Two half-square triangles create quiet areas.

Block 2: Quarter-square triangles add interest.

Blending a soft edge You can use just a portion of the circle to add interest to the quilt. The soft edge (see Glossary, page 76) encourages the viewer to look carefully at your quilt. For a soft edge to be effective it should be a surprise to discover that the whole circle is actually there. Most of the circle edges should be high contrast, or easily seen. Block 3 has a green triangle that enhances the greens in the circle and retains the same value as the triangle it replaced. The value flow of the block is maintained even with a change in color. Value is more important than color.

Block 3: the importance of value

Block 4 has four quarter-square triangles that form the background square. The dark, medium, dark, medium value arrangement makes it difficult to develop a smooth value flow through all the blocks. It is better to switch the two quarter-square triangles to create a smoother medium, medium, dark, dark flow in Block 5.

Block 4: Dark, medium, dark, medium value flow is difficult to blend with the background.

Block 5: Medium, medium, dark, dark allows a smooth value flow.

Block 6 is the final choice. The medium-green fabric with textural lines has the potential to flow to the next block. The small, textured triangle blends with the circle and encourages the lines from the circle to continue into the background triangle lines. The two dark, busy textured triangles have been enlarged to one half-square triangle, soft edging half of the circle. The large dark half-square triangle uses the dark line of the circle to disguise the diagonal seamline of the background block.

Block 6: Final fabric choices

Consider using one of two methods for cutting the background triangles
Using Omnigrid rulers makes the cutting quick and accurate. Both the half-square triangle (#96L) and the quarter-square triangle (#98L) rulers include the seam allowance so the numbers on the rulers are the cut size, not the finished size (see Glossary, page 76). Using the ruler to cut a 6" triangle will make a 6" triangle plus the seam allowance. Both rulers have numbers printed on the outside grainline of the triangle. With the #98L ruler the largest quarter-square triangle you can cut will fit a 12" block. The #96L ruler can cut a half-square triangle for up to an 8" block.

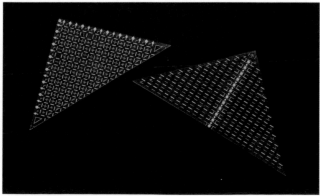

Omnigrid rulers #96L and #98L

Make your own plastic templates to cut larger blocks (9" and up). After you make the templates, mark them with a permanent marker to indicate the block size, grainlines, and type of triangle: half- or quarter-square. It is helpful to mark the seamline perimeter with ¼" masking tape or fine-tip permanent pen. Using plastic templates enables you to see the design lines of the fabric through the plastic.

Design components The design from the circle connects with the circular design in the background fabric. To define the best background triangle to cut use the quarter-square plastic template. Place the half-square triangle template in position to check that the circle placement will not be too far off the "page" over the outside edge of the block. You can also check if the circular design line would flow more easily onto a quarter-square triangle or a half-square triangle. The fourth photo shows the potential for error: making a cut so high that the circle will not fit onto the opposite edge of the block.

Circle connects with the circular design in the background.

Use the half-square triangle to check the fit of the circle and block.

Is the flow better with a half-square triangle or quarter-square triangle?

Oops! The circle won't fit the background block.

Cut and construct the block To continue the triangle's design line from one block to the next, carefully cut the triangle to align the desired line. Place the quarter-square triangle template for the adjacent block and notice the overlapping seam allowance for the two seamlines.

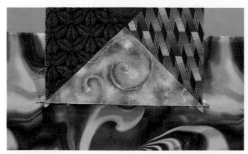

Desired line

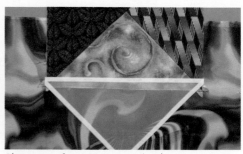

Placement of quarter-square triangle

Move the completed block out of the way to cut the triangle with the template in the correct place. Blocks designed as a pair need to be kept together to maintain the design-line flow when we smooth the arrangement in Chapter 4.

Cutting position for adjacent triangle

ADD INTEREST WITH STRIPES

Striped fabrics can add interest if you choose a narrow, low-contrast stripe. (see *Circles I*, page 13). However, a wide, dramatic striped fabric in a half-square triangle might be very distracting. When stripes are used in a half-square triangle, one outside-edge stripe will either be parallel to the block edge (miter corner), while one stripe will be perpendicular to the block edge (chevron corner). Check either the chevron or miter effect by folding the striped fabric into four layers, then folding back the first two layers to form a 45° angle.

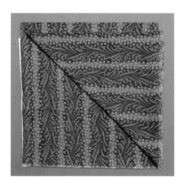

Fold fabric to audition stripes.

To cut either the chevron or the miter, fold the striped fabric over itself in the direction of the stripe. Position the quarter-square triangle template, as in the photos, to cut the type of corner seam for your block. Cut both layers of the striped fabric at the same time. A matched miter or chevron will form when the triangles are sewn together.

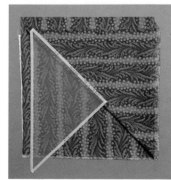

The template is positioned to miter the stripe in the half-square triangle.

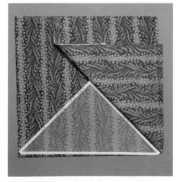

The template is positioned to cut a chevron for the half-square triangle.

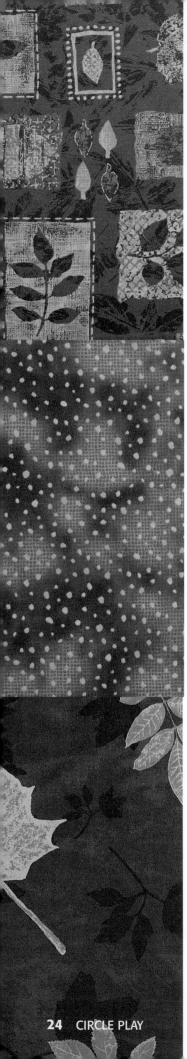

Template position to cut a miter corner seam

Template position to cut a chevron corner seam

Completed mitered corner

Completed chevron corner

Sewing and Pressing

Before removing a background block from the design wall, mark the orientation (which side is up). I use either a vertical pin or a dot sticker to indicate the top. Carry the block pieces (the triangles) to the sewing machine on a flat surface (a sheet of paper or a cutting board) to keep the orientation of the pieces intact. Use the block's assigned circle for a final check at the machine before stitching. This final check with the circle can prevent a reversal of the two smaller triangles.

Designing each square for its circle assumes the block can now be pieced. After sewing, press each seam open to keep the block as flat as possible. The subsequent circles will be flat when used in a second generation quilt. See *Circles II*, page 64 to see the circles reclaimed from the background blocks of *Circles I*, page 13 (more on this in Chapter 7).

Pin the circle to the completed background block, matching the design lines of the circle to the planned seamlines and/or design lines of the fabrics used in the block.

Tip

When aligning the design lines of the circle to the seamlines of the block the relationship between the circle and its background block, in terms of value and line, is more important than traditional centering.

When the circles are pinned to the background block the freezer paper is covered up. Don't worry; after the individual blocks are completed, their arrangement is finalized, and the circles are appliquéd, the background fabric will be carefully trimmed away, and the freezer paper can be removed.

Read This Before You Move on to the Next Chapter

Before you move on to Chapter 4, Composing Circle Quilts, there are two things you should think about.

First, I recommend stitching the blocks together at this point, even though some triangles may need to be replaced in the final composition (more about that later). Sew the blocks together so you can easily rotate them on the design wall to control the value flow across the quilt. Stitching the block also eliminates the distracting seam allowances and places the focus on the design flow. If the thought of ripping seams is less than appealing, I suggest these alternative methods:

- Pin the background triangles into place on a square of paper before pinning on the circle. Pin from behind to be less visually distracting.
  Or . . .
- Iron the triangles to a square of freezer paper before pinning the circles. These two alternatives are quicker, but the focus of the block will be less sharp because of the distracting seam allowances.

Second, the careful planning and implementing of the fabric design-line flow from circle to texture line of the block, or texture lines from block to block, are special to both the quilter and the viewer. If design-line flow is used at all it should be used sparingly. It is enough if it happens once or twice in a quilt, rewarding the viewer with the "Aha!" of discovery. I call this the "Cinderella effect."

Cinderella would not have been so beautiful if she wasn't surrounded by her ugly stepsisters, just as your quilt would not be as intriguing if this design-line flow happened in or between each block in the quilt.

INDONESIAN CIRCLES, 36" x 36", by Reynola Pakusich. This quilt demonstrates how using one traditional Indonesian batik for the circles can alter the implied seamlines of the block to the circle. The quilting in the border follows the design of the second piece of batik. Background blocks use commercial fabrics chosen primarily for their value, tone, density, and size rather than mood; notice the grape-leaf print of the triangle on the right side of the center.

TROPICAL LEAF CIRCLES II, 33" x 46", by Suzanne Keeney Lucy. This second-generation quilt takes advantage of the transparency effect between circles and background.

Value Flow, Smooth Moves

The three teaching samples in this chapter illustrate value flow across the background quilt in combination with the circles.

TEACHING SAMPLE 1

In Teaching Sample 1 the circles and backgrounds are designed as a unit. The block units are then rearranged, rotated, and some background triangles are even replaced, in an effort to enhance the value flow across the quilt.

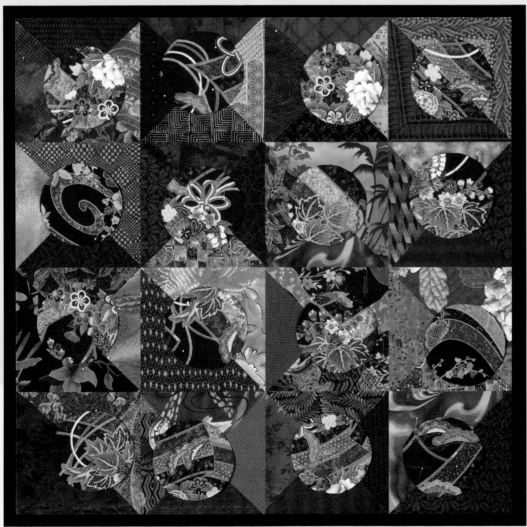

Teaching Sample 1: blocks placed randomly on the design wall

Smoothing the value flow involves fine-tuning the transition from light to dark value movement across the quilt blocks. Smoothing can be done in two directions: darkening a too-light area or lightening a too-dark area. A half-square triangle can seem too heavy, even with the right value, and needs to be exchanged with two quarter-square triangles, one of which is the original fabric. One side of a half-square triangle may fail to blend or flow to the next block and can be replaced with two quarter-square ones. Compare the triangles that were replaced to smooth the value flow.

Replace triangles to smooth the value flow.

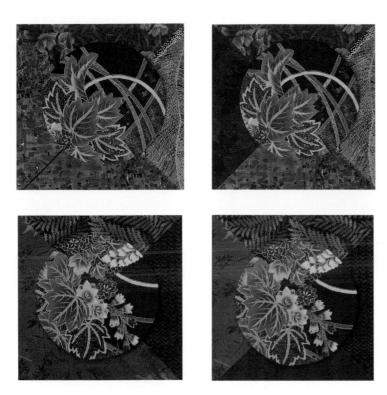

It takes less than five minutes to replace a stitched triangle. With a seam ripper, break every three or four stitches in the replacement area plus ½" beyond. On the reverse side of the seam, break the stitching at the end of the area to be ripped. That seamline can now be easily and gently pulled out, leaving the fabrics with very little distortion.

Teaching Sample 1: final version with improved value flow

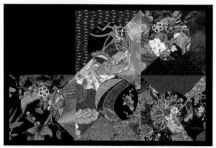

You can continue to experiment with the blocks of Teaching Sample 1 to outline value flow, fill it in, and refine it. Try placing the darkest blocks in a diagonal line. With the addition of the remaining blocks the dark line might be turned or altered at either end.

Here the lightest blocks are arranged together before adding the rest of the blocks.

Darkest blocks form a diagonal line.

Lightest blocks set together.

Darkest blocks in left corner

Another option is to place the darkest blocks together in the lower-left corner before working the remaining blocks toward the upper-right corner of the quilt.

Here the blocks from Teaching Sample 1 are set on point. You'll need two more blocks to complete this design layout. The value flow forms rectangles and squares that interlock and change. While you smooth the value flow try to keep the blocks together where the design flows from block to block (see page 12). You may discover additional places where the design lines flow from one block to another. In the examples above there are several light background triangles around the outside edge of the center field.

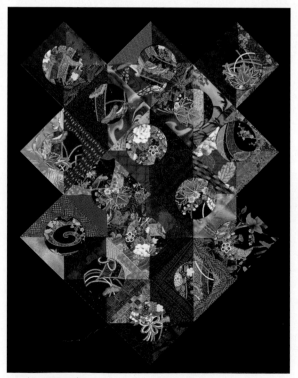

The entire value flow of the center field does not need to be enclosed. Enclosure is the function of the borders, which is discussed in Chapter 5. The light triangles on the outside of the perimeter have the potential to integrate the center field (see Glossary, page 76) of the quilt with the border.

Teaching Sample 1 with the blocks set on point

LATTICE STRIPS

Each setting example might benefit from the addition of lattice strips.

The dark lattice in the example below adds depth without interfering with the line and value flow from block to block. This additional depth is some of the excitement, magic, and mystery of quilt designing.

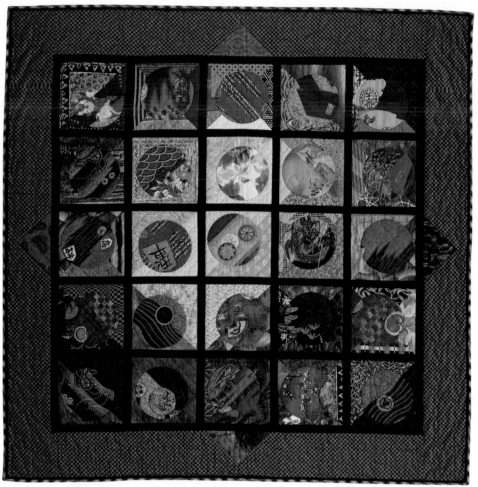

JAPANESE CIRCLES 1, 44" x 47" by Reynola Pakusich

Teaching Sample 2

Designed with only two fabrics, the entire background of Teaching Sample 2 was composed before the circles were added. With careful fabric selection the interaction of circle-to-block can still occur, though probably less often than in Teaching Sample 1 (but with no less excitement!).

If you use one fabric for the circles it should feature several colors as before, with right angles repeated throughout the design.

Once the right angles in the fabric are identified, audition a circle size that emphasizes the right-angle corner of the circle. For the print on page 33, a 3⅛" circle window template (traced around a coffee mug) showed the right angle more clearly than a 2½" window (traced around a water glass). The circle fabric is an all over print, so the 16 circles can be cut randomly, 4 layers at a time, before ironing on the freezer-paper circles. Teaching Sample 2 used two-thirds of a yard for the circles.

Multicolored fabrics with right angles

One yard of this hand-dyed background fabric repeats the colors of the circle fabric, though not in the same proportions. Because these triangles are all from the same fabric it is efficient to fold the yard into four layers and cut four strips 5 7/8" wide. Cut these strips into 5 7/8" x 5 7/8" squares, then cut the squares diagonally in half into triangles. Use these to make 5" finished background blocks. Cut an additional 6 1/4" square from the folded fabric. Cut this square twice diagonally into quarter-square triangles for the 5" finished block. Now you have enough triangles to start designing the background.

I began designing Teaching Sample 2 by arranging 16 of the half-square triangles as the lower-left corners of the 16 background blocks. This identified the shape and perimeter of the piece.

Shape and perimeter of Teaching Sample 2

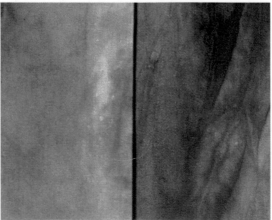

Support fabric for Teaching Sample 2

Fabric for Teaching Sample 2 circles

The upper-right corners of the background blocks were filled in as I placed the colors in zones (see Glossary, page 76). At this point 13 of the 16 blocks were made up of 2 half-square triangles while 3 blocks were composed of 3 triangles (1 half-square and 2 quarter-square) each. The composition was smoothed, fine-tuning the transition, value, and color flow between the blocks while creating a strong central diagonal line from upper-left to lower-right. The background blocks were further refined by expanding the blue triangles and smoothing the transitions. Compare the placement of the background blocks from the loosely defined perimeter to the final block placement, below.

This smoothing process can result in some leftover triangles as the heavy triangles were weeded out. A few of them might be used as part of the border, or they can be used to create a pieced back for the project. See Chapter 6, page 51.

Notice how well the 16 circles fit onto the seamlines of the blocks. Part of this fit is the successful selection of the circle fabric. Most of this fitting is the result of developing the ability to see fabric designs in new ways.

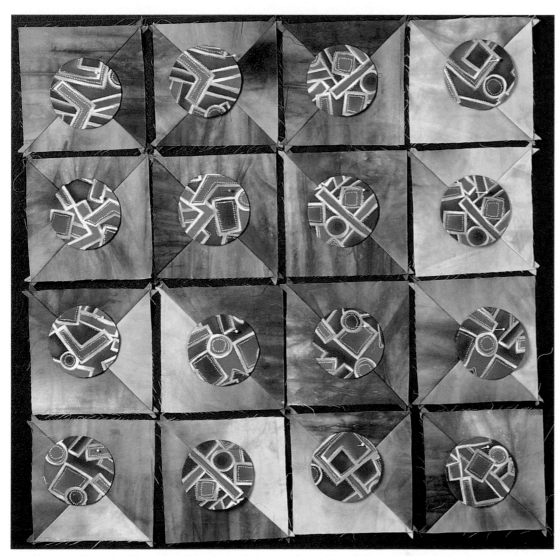

Teaching Sample 2: The right angles of the design fit the seamlines of the blocks and the background is smoothed after some blue triangles are replaced.

Teaching Sample 3

With Teaching Sample 3 you reverse the process and group, or zone, the 16 circles *first* before working out the background as a whole. I grouped the circles so the light values are in the upper-left and the dark values are in the lower-right.

Two of the circles were exchanged to keep the lightest area inside the perimeter. In this set of leaf circles the green moves not only in value from light to dark, but also in clarity and intensity from muted soft tones to darker clear tones.

Circles zoned by value

BACKGROUND BLOCKS

Place the background blocks. The photo below shows the beginning of the background with the first circle in place.

Curves in the leaf print (upper-left) are reflected by the textural flow of the circle.

Even when you separate the two design processes—circles and background— the integration lines can still be developed. The design lines of the circle can be related to the seamlines of the block, and to design lines in the background blocks.

Teaching Sample 3: Blocks on the design wall

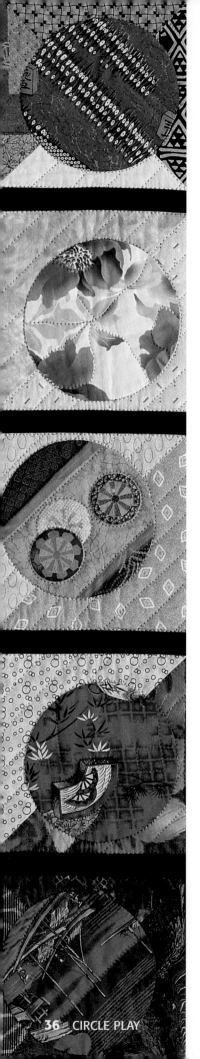

Sewing the Circles to the Blocks

Once the center field (see Glossary, page 76) is completed in any of the teaching samples, the circles are ready to be sewn to the blocks. Before removing any block from the design wall, mark the top of each block, the row, and its position in the row. I use vertical pins or dot stickers. You spent a lot of time creating the blocks and their positions. Without knowing the top of the block, there are at least three ways to return it to the wall in the wrong position!

This is your final chance to check the orientation of the circle to its background block. You should do two things:

1. Make sure the design lines of the circle meet the seamlines of the block.
2. Check that the design lines from the circle match the design lines of the triangles as planned.

Place a pin at each of these critical junctions. If the spacing is a tiny bit off, sometimes I "fudge," allowing a bit of fullness in the background to make the design lines meet. The fullness can be camouflaged by the batting or by the quilting process. (In my grandmother's era the saying was "It will quilt out." I can personally justify this procedure for design lines more than I can for sloppy stitching or cutting.)

If you discover a misjudgment after stitching the circles to the blocks, all is not lost. The gray printed circle band was meant to align with the darker gray portion of the triangle. I stitched it (viewing it close up) at the wrong edge of the gray circle band. The more I looked at it I realized the gray band was wrong. Because the circle fabric is fine wool I hesitated to rip it out and re-orient the circle. To reduce the impact I used a Pigma pen to shade the space on the triangle next to the circle, and signed my name. By darkening one area I diminished the glaring light space.

Fudging a misjudgment using a Pigma pen

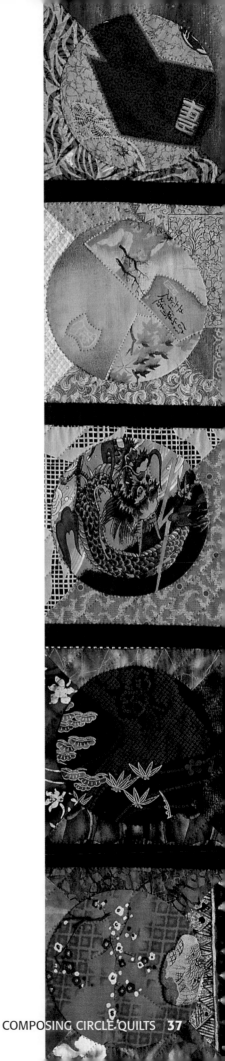

Fine-tune your quilt over several days, and at different times of the day. Room lighting changes and affects what you see during the day. Experiment in the evening by turning on and off various room lights. Check the composition using only a hall light or light from the next room. Check your work from a distance using a reducing glass, a small door peephole (check your local hardware store), or looking through the large end of your binoculars. A camera allows a different view of the piece. Your friends' or spouse's input can be valuable because they do not "own" the work and do not have a vested interest in it. Fresh opinions are valuable; non-quilters may not be able to say how to fix it but they can often identify a problem area.

When aligning the circles to the background blocks by line, value, and sometimes texture, these elements become more important to the whole quilt than the figures of the patterned fabric. In the photo below the circle value, line, and texture blend well with the background block and neighboring blocks. The figure is actually an upside-down lion. This allows the viewer to participate in the quilt by mentally reversing the lion.

The design lines and texture of the lion are visually more important than the actual image or its orientation.

OPTIONS FOR SEWING

You can sew the circles onto the blocks using hand appliqué, a machine blind-hem stitch, or topstitching them by machine. Galleries include quilts using each of these methods. I prefer to hand appliqué the circles using a neutral color (dark, medium, or light value) silk thread because the stitching shows the least. The top-stitching on the circles of Annette Anderson's *Japanese Ladies* (page 8) does not distract from the beauty of the quilt lines at all.

CUTTING AWAY BACKGROUND FABRIC

After the circles are stitched to the blocks, remove the freezer paper and excess background fabric from behind the circle. Turn the block over to see the circle stitching line. Carefully cut through the block fabric starting about ¼" inside the circle. If this is your first time trimming behind an appliqué it can be scary. Two words of encouragement: the tips of your scissors will let you feel the freezer paper, and if you should actually cut through the circle fabric all is not lost. A circle patch can be a wonderful design feature. If you use a circle patch, be sure to add a couple more so it reads "design" instead of "accident."

Reduce bulky seam allowances If the trimming results in excess bulk, you may want to reduce the seam allowances by cutting the block seam allowance a hair narrower than the gathered circle seam allowance.

You can use some of the cut-away circles in the current quilt in the block design, as circle patches mentioned above, or in the border design. See *Asilomar Circles I* (page 63) and *Moonlight* (page 61).

True-up the blocks Because the piecing and appliquéing steps sometimes distort the work, you can now true-up (see Glossary, page 76) each block. First press each block carefully with a dry iron and identify the smallest block. The size or shape distortion may be only ¹⁄₁₆" off but will make a difference in how flat the quilt finishes. Cut a square of freezer paper the cut size of the finished block. I usually need to remove about ⅛" from two sides, in an L shape. This seems to be my personal distortion amount for machine stitching.

Center the freezer paper over the back of the block and iron the freezer-paper square to the back of each block in turn, carefully matching the corners with each seamline of the triangles. The block fabric should at least touch all edges of the paper. Using a rotary cutter and ruler trim off any excess fabric. Remove the paper and true-up the remainder of the blocks. If you are working with nine or more blocks, replace the square of freezer paper every two or three blocks; the paper gradually shrinks, even when you use a dry iron.

Freezer-paper template for truing-up the blocks

Once the blocks are squared, carefully stitch them together into rows. Press the seams *open* to keep the work flat. Join the rows to complete the center field. Pressed-open seams reduce bulk at the corners (where as many as eight fabrics may meet). Return the piece to your design wall for Chapter 5: Adding Borders.

5 Adding Borders

Congratulations! You finished your first *Circle Play* quilt top and are wondering whether or not to add borders. Let's consider some possible options for borders.

AFRICAN CIRCLES II, 34" x 34", by Reynola Pakusich.

ATOMIUM, 26" x 32", by Gladys Love. The curved borders integrate beautifully with the circles, creating new border shapes. The use of appliqué fish blending into the background curves and values makes the viewer search further for the fish parts of the circle fabrics.

This chapter focuses on Teaching Sample 4, with a nine-block center field. The five border options, or parts of them, are found in many of the finished quilts in the following chapters and the Galleries.

Look for potential design clues in the center field. An uneven number of blocks suggests placing the center field on point. There are three value flows from upper-left to lower-right, and one dark value flow from upper-right to lower-left. The three light triangles on the top, left, and lower edges offer areas to expand the center field into the border. Teaching Sample 4 provides hints for a second-generation quilt. Look at the two circles forming rings or doughnuts in the center-left and center-bottom rows. See how the design lines continue through circles, block to block, flowing through the next circle onto a seamline.

Teaching Sample 4: Nine-block center field

Design-line flow

Border Option 1: Four Triangles

EXPAND THE DESIGN FROM THE CENTER FIELD INTO THE BORDER

You can use triangles to expand the design from the center field. An additional layer appears—a square on point behind the nine blocks. Move the four triangles to the opposite two corners and the layer behind the blocks becomes a rectangle.

On-point square appears behind the center field.

Diagonal rectangle appears behind the center field.

Triangles at the end of a value flow bring that value flow into the border. Value is what's critical here, more than matching fabric prints, colors, or even balancing the triangles on the sides of the center field. The quilts on pages 31, and 63–65 show other ways to use quarter-square triangles in the border.

Once I decided to use the four dark triangles, fabric was needed to finish the borders. I used a half yard of lengthwise striped fabric cut the same width as the height of the triangle plus ⅛".

Triangles move the light flow into the border.

Fabric strips finish the border. A generous strip allows for mitering.

CONSTRUCTING THE BORDER

To construct the border, cut a 45° angle on one end of the striped border fabric and stitch it to one side of the triangle using the usual ¼" seam allowance. Cut a reverse (135°) angle on another border strip and sew it to the other side of the triangle. Press the seam allowances open to help them lay flat. Seam allowances pressed toward the border strips help the four triangles recede slightly from the center field. This reinforces the illusion of an additional layer. Leave a generous amount of the border strip at each end to miter the corners. Notice the miter in the upper-left corner. Mitered corners are important as a design feature because they continue the on-point effect of the quarter-square triangles.

The next border completes the "picture" because it repeats the value of the center field. This outer border may be too wide, but once the seams are stitched and the piece is more in focus the border can be narrowed. Sew the two borders together and then miter each corner with a single seam for a smooth frame.

Border option 1: Teaching Sample 4. Compare the look of the mitered corner in the upper left corner to the stacked corners. The dark outer border repeats the value of the center field.

AUDITIONING WELTS

Adding a welt (see Glossary, page 76) is useful in many of the Circle Play quilts. The small size of the welt can add an effective amount of bright, light, or dark accent where a triangle with the same value or intensity would be overwhelming.

The welt being auditioned in the next example is a ¼" folded welt. Similar to a double mat on a picture, the welt can serve to increase the depth between the center field and the border. The welt also repeats the design lines of the center blocks.

Fabric choices for the welt often read as a solid or are geometric rather than busy florals. Narrow stripes work well as a cross-stripe cut or a bias cut, rather than lengthwise stripes which tend to wander out of line when stitched.

Making the welt To make the welt, cut 4 strips 1" wide by the length of each side. If a side requires more than one length, piece it on the diagonal as shown to reduce bulk. Press the welt strips in half lengthwise with right sides out.

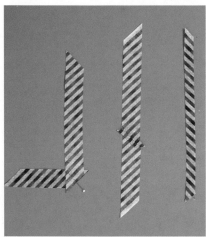

Join and press a bias welt.

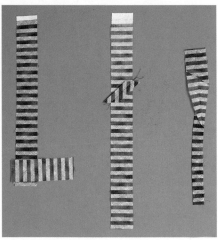

Join and press a cross-strip welt.

Pressing the welt toward the center field

The welt fold The welt can fold either toward or away from the center field. When the welt folds toward the center field it more closely resembles the double mat of a framed picture. This option will cover the tips of the triangles along the edge of the center field. Sew the welt strips onto the quilt top in a top/bottom and side/side sequence. You are stitching narrow strips to make ¼" finished welts, so wobbly stitching will show up easily. To avoid this problem use the folded edge as your sewing guide for the ¼" seam allowance, rather than the usual cut edges, if your presser foot is ¼" on both sides of the needle.

Pin and sew the next border to the quilt. With the back of the quilt facing up, you can stitch on the previous welt seamline to maintain an accurate welt width. When stitching on the outer border, stitch seamline to seamline rather than cut-edge to cut-edge so the corners can be mitered. In other words, stop and start your stitching ¼" away from the cut edges.

If the welt is pressed away from the center field the triangles tips are exposed but you'll need to prepare the ends of the welt strips. Pin the welt to the quilt to double-check the finished length. Fold back each end, allowing a seam allowance on both the welt and the pieced area. Trim the welt on the diagonal to reduce bulk. Remove the welt strip and press lengthwise with right sides out. Re-pin the welt to the quilt edges and stitch down the center of the strip using the folded side as the ¼" seam allowance. The ends of the welt strip stop ¼" from the quilt edge. Add the next border as before. Before mitering the corners of the outer borders make sure the folded ends of the welt form the notch as shown.

The border is folded to form a mitered corner. The welt is pressed away from the center field. Notice the notch at the corner of the welt.

Border Option 2: Dancing in Center Field

The second border treatment places the center field askew to add movement, making it seem to dance! It is important for the outside edges of the long triangles to be on the straight grain.

Border Option 2: Teaching Sample 4 with a 5" border

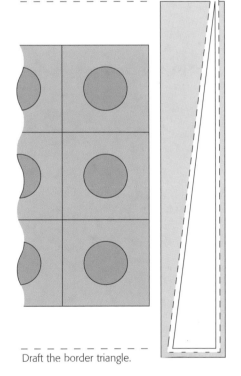

Draft the border triangle.

To draft a pattern for this triangle border piece, draw a rectangle on newsprint the finished length of the center field plus *twice* the finished width of the borders. Draw a diagonal line on the rectangle from lower-right to upper- left. Add ¼" seam allowance around the three sides of the triangle to make the border pattern piece. Make a dot at the seam allowance on the narrow tip of the triangle to match the corners when stitching.

For triangle borders all four layers of the border fabric need to be right side up. I cut four strips of the border fabric, press them flat, and stack them face up. I place the pattern on top of the four layers, and cut out the triangle. The border triangles will be stitched onto the center field, Log Cabin style, in a counterclockwise order. Take a look at Tomoko Yoshihashi's *Moonlight* (page 61) in which she takes this border treatment even further.

Border Option 3: Bands of Value

The third border treatment explores the effects of bands of value flowing from the center field out into the border.

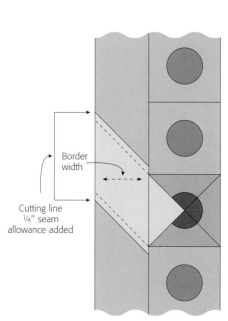

Border
width

Cutting line
¼" seam
allowance added

Draft the parallelogram for
the border strip.

Border Option 3: Teaching Sample 4, Auditioning borders with value flow

Cut these border strips the height of the quarter-square triangle plus ⅛". Audition them the same way the center field was fine-tuned—over a period of time, with a variety of lighting, using tools such as a camera, and soliciting opinions from family members and friends.

Notice the high contrast of the quarter-square triangle with the dark border in the upper-right. Now the corner seems to glow with depth. The other two light values in the border extend the light flow. Try turning the ends of the border strips in the opposite direction from the light flows for an unexpected effect. The cutting challenge here is the parallelograms of the two light border pieces. Easy solution: Measure the finished size of the block, and add a seam allowance on each end of the border piece using the 45° angle.

Use the same method to measure and create border pieces that may be as long as three pieced blocks of the center field. Look for these shapes, with the ends angled in the opposite direction as the center field value flow, in the border treatment of *Circles, III* (page 64).

Border Option 4: Floating Triangles

The next quilt, *Japanese Circles I* (page 31), uses a solid inner border and a triangle that is floating (see Glossary, page 76) in an outer border.

Border detail from **JAPANESE CIRCLES I**

Border detail for a floating triangle

The quarter-square triangle extends the value flow from the center field into the border. The triangle can appear to float in front of or behind the black inner border. The sewing sequence of the border pieces determines its appearance. In *Japanese Circles I* the inner black border was sewn onto the center field first, then the outer border with the quarter-square triangle, was added.

In *African Circles II* (page 39) the dark inner border was sewn to the long outer border strip before the 45° angle was cut and the quarter-square triangle was attached. The quarter-square triangle that extends into the border will appear to float if the last border extends beyond the peak of the triangle. See if you can figure out how this was done in the following photo.

Border detail from **AFRICAN CIRCLES II**

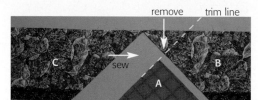

Sew A to B. Trim and remove the excess. Sew C to A/B.

The quarter-square triangle can be stitched to one border piece, which will align the lower edges of the triangle with the right side of the border strip. Stitch and press the seam open, then trim the excess border strip by extending the angle of the other short side of the triangle. This piece will now fit the other length of the side border strip. Follow the same process with the other border design.

Border Option 5

Audition fabrics for the border designing process For Teaching Sample 2 I auditioned a black and white irregular, striped welt, a narrow strip of fuchsia to strengthen the fuchsia color from the theme print, and a wider strip of theme fabric for the outer border. Try a black binding to frame this very bright and wild quilt.

Think about potential backing, binding, and quilting patterns during the designing process to integrate each of the components of the quilt. Let's move on to the final steps to complete your *Circle Play* quilt.

Teaching Sample 2 (page 33) border possibilities

REYNOLA'S CIRCLES #3, 18" x 18", by Pat Mead. The narrow, floating, black band in the border and the double lattice that weaves at the block intersections enhance the oriental fabrics and create a wonderful unity of design.

ELEMENTS OF DESIGN, 90½" x 116½", by Aileen Brock. The number of blocks in this full-size quilt allows wonderful value play behind the circles. The reversed value placement of the pieced border reflects that value flow.

Generations of Circles

Here's proof that one quilt leads to another. See page 72 for another series related to these quilts.

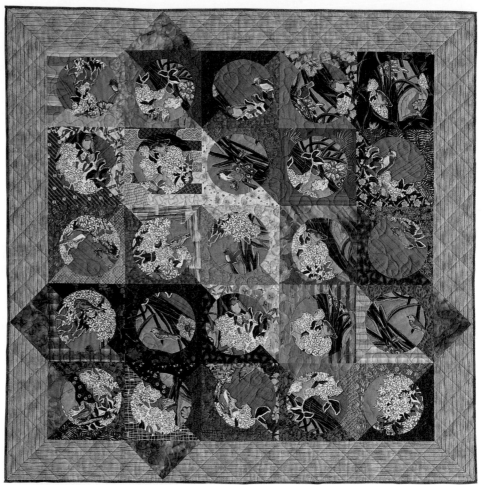

FIRST GENERATION EARTHTONES, 52" x 52", by Cory Volkert. Variation in density and line in the circle fabrics allows greater variety of the background blocks.

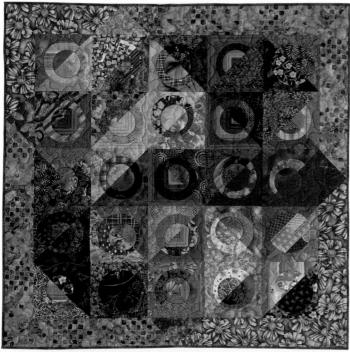

SECOND GENERATION EARTHTONES, 43" x 43", by Cory Volkert. The rings of the circles turn from soft to hard edges across the surface of light, creating a gently mysterious whole. The border fabric texture leads the viewer to the next quilt.

THIRD GENERATION EARTHTONES, 43" x 43", by Cory Volkert. Here the artist used circles from both previous quilts that seem to float on a checkered background. The undulating strips gracefully form the focus for the background movement.

6 Finishing Touches

Now that your quilt top is complete, you are ready to discover the design choices for the backing, quilting, and binding.

Backing

The back of the quilt offers an opportunity to surprise the viewer. It can relate in color, design, and mood to the quilt top. The back can be treated as a more relaxed design area in a larger scale. Here is a chance to experiment with leftover pieces of the fabrics used in the front.

When hand quilting, I like to use lighter-weight yardage, which makes smaller stitches less difficult. I often use a plaid fabric because it is easier to cut the larger pieces on grain. If the quilt will be machine quilted, used on a bed, or is for a child, I use regular quilt-weight cottons or sometimes an irresistible piece of decorator fabric.

I often force myself to piece the back of the quilt. For backing fabrics I usually buy two to four yards, which I know will not be enough for a full-sized quilt. Even when making smaller quilts the top seems to be barely larger than the backing fabric. It has been fun to solve these "problems" in a visually pleasing manner.

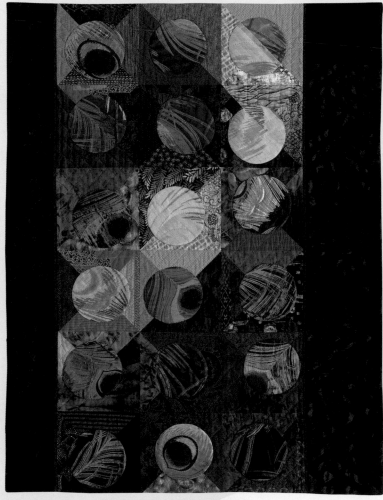

OBI CIRCLES I, 35½" x 46½", by Reynola Pakusich.

Fabric width The width of the fabric is the most common problem. Wash, iron, and fold your yardage lengthwise into four layers in preparation. To adjust the fabric width, I suggest cutting the backing fabric lengthwise at the quarter fold. Separate the two lengthwise pieces so they are far enough apart for the width of the quilt, including 4"–6" of extension allowances. The resulting space is a creative, practical area for design. Arrange the leftover triangles from the front in a design value flow or as pinwheels to fill in this area. Center the blocks and use a single fabric to complete the border strip above and below the blocks. The blocks won't be cut off when you trim the outside edges of the quilt for binding, or covered by the hanging sleeve. You can also add a strip or panel of contrasting fabric in an unexpected color or design.

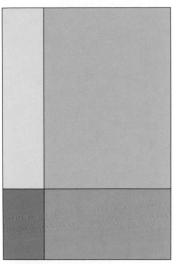

Potential design areas

What if your backing fabric isn't long enough? Cut across the full width of the fabric about three-fourths of the fabric length. Add fabrics here to create the necessary length (plus 4"–6" extension allowances). Then cut the length of the backing on the quarter fold, rotate the narrower strip, and sew it to the larger piece of the backing. The back of the quilt looks less haphazard, and is much more interesting.

To add to both the length and width of the quilt backing, insert the added width first, the lengthwise design, before adding the needed length, or horizontal design. This sequence keeps your added design areas more intact. These are only two of many possible solutions, and are meant as a springboard for your own creative problem solving.

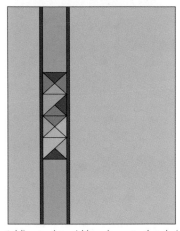

Adding to the width only; note the dark "spacer" strips flanking the pieced area.

Batting Choices

Quilt batting choices depend on the desired appearance of the quilt, quilting decisions, and end use of the quilt. I use a thin batting such as Thermore (which is designed for clothing) when hand quilting because it creates comfortable drapiness which I prefer, and allows for smaller stitches. When planning to machine quilt, a slightly heavier batting such as the thinnest of all-cotton or Quilters Dream Cotton Request Loft balances the effect of the machine stitching while still creating the quilting texture.

Basting

You can baste a quilt sandwich—the quilt top, batting, and backing—in many different ways. I like to use a spray-basting adhesive because it is quick, easy, and produces a smooth result. This process works best with four or six hands. It is worth waiting to collect fellow quilters with their own quilts that need to be basted.

Press the quilt top and backing. Make sure all seams are laying in the desired direction. Open the batting to a single layer; let it relax for about an hour. Cut the batting about 3"–4" larger than the quilt top on all sides. Layer and baste as desired.

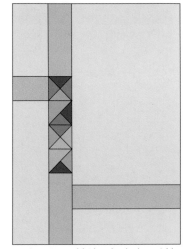

Design area added to both the width and length.

Quilting Designs

Tip

Be careful not to mix chalk and pen because heat and steam may set some chalk colors!

There are two basic goals for quilting designs and variations. The practical goal is to fasten the three layers of the quilt sandwich together with an even density of quilting. The visually exciting goal is to enhance and perhaps blend the action of the circles with the background value and color play.

To keep the marking to a minimum you can use various widths of masking tape and rulers (or a folded piece of paper with a 45° angle) to eliminate marking the top. Chalk works well for marking, if needed, because it will usually brush off. I keep a dry washcloth handy to remove the chalk before changing the quilting hoop to another section of the quilt. It seems easier to remove chalk marks while the layers are taut in the hoop. As the tension of the hoop is released, the chalk is embedded into the fabric. The White Marking Pen (fine) from Clover is my current favorite because it makes a fine line and can be removed with heat and/or steam from the iron.

Quilting designs First consider the theme of the circles. Study what is going on in the circle, the movement of the design lines within the circle, and how the line movement can be enhanced. Plan to avoid the bulk of the seams with the quilting stitches. Design lines of the circles provide obvious quilting clues: repeating the dominant lines, or echo quilting.

Here are other details of possible quilting designs.

AFRICAN CIRCLES I Repeating the dominant lines

AFRICAN CIRCLES I Echo quilting

TROPICAL LEAF CIRCLE 1 The leaf design flows from the circle into the background

Note the beige block in **JAPANESE CIRCLES I.**

In **CIRCLES I** the quilting lines disregard texture lines.

In the example below the fan section is outlined and three quilted arcs are added to imply a sphere rather than a flat surface.

Tip

Avoid over-quilting; a few lines are enough. If you quilt too close together the circle will be flat.

CIRCLES 1 The circle design is blended with the quilting lines, the three quilted arcs and the outline-quilted fan secton.

Keep the background in mind as you select quilting designs. The simplest approach is to use diagonal lines for the background quilting. In *Circles I* (page 13) the entire pieced background is diagonally quilted (upper-right to lower-left), the edge of the center field is quilted, and then the diagonal quilting line is reversed for the borders. This is simple, effective, and requires few decisions.

Mark the grid lines with masking tape from corner to opposite corner. The straight lines of the background create a pleasing contrast to the curves of the circles.

Japanese Circles I and *Obi Circles I* (pages 31 and 50) take the diagonal line idea a step further by following the value flow of the pieced block background behind the outlined latticing.

A third suggestion is to quilt the background with curves using a template. I am delighted with how well a 60° sashiko (see Glossary, page 76) design fits as a background grid on *African Circles II* (page 39).

In some of the second- and third-generation quilts, the circles have been outlined (see *Circles II*, page 64). In *Japanese Circles II* (page 66) the rings are emphasized by quilted diagonal grids through the middle of the circle ring.

A combination of these quilting ideas is shown in *Vert Coterie* (page 5); the X-shaped value flow is quilted diagonally and the background is quilted with a sashiko stencil.

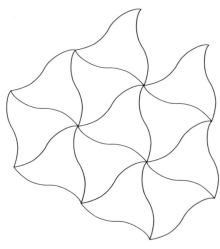

Stem Source International quilting design

TROPICAL LEAF CIRCLE I, 35½" x 36", by Suzanne Keeney Lucy. Notice how the quilting integrates the circle theme with the background.

Japanese Connecting Plover quilting design

BORDERS

A change of diagonal line direction or parallel lines for the quilting works well for borders. You can also break up the border by extending the triangular lines of the blocks. Study the borders in *Vert Coterie* (page 5) and *Asilomar Circles I* (page 63) for other variations. Sometimes the border quilting simply needs to follow the fabric pattern as in *Obi Circles I* (see page 50).

In *Plaid Circles I* the quilting reverses the relationship between the straight lines of plaids/stripes and the curves of circles. Quilting around the circles lifts them, and the quilting lines within the circles continue the lines of the triangles in the background blocks. The background Japanese Connecting Plover is a traditional sashiko design found in many Japanese textile books. It's a good pattern to repeat the circle curves on top of the straight lines of plaids, to create a juxtaposition of motion. The border quilting repeats the triangle lines from the background blocks on the wavy curve of the printed tone-on-tone texture of the black border fabric.

PLAID CIRCLES I, 35" x 35", by Reynola Pakusich. This quilt uses a large variety of plaid fabrics—varying in size, density, and value—for the circles. The quilting lines in the circles follow the seamlines of the blocks, more closely unifying the quilt.

For hand quilting, I use a long, thin, size 12 needle to achieve a smaller stitch. The eye of the needle is small, so use a thin quilting thread. The value of the color is more important than the thread color. *African Circles I* (page 8) was quilted with lime-green thread, which is less noticeable than the texture of the quilting lines.

Basting the quilt sandwich with spray adhesive allows you to begin quilting in any area. I quilt the circles first so I have time to think about background and borders. A 14" round hoop is useful for the circles. On the smaller quilts this hoop will allow two circles to be quilted before moving to the next area. I use an oval hoop for the larger background area, or quilt the background and borders on a large floor frame. The quilting process, especially hand quilting, is quietly soothing and allows the quiltmaker to begin thinking about the next step, the binding.

Tip

Pin a folded dishtowel to the edge of the quilt top to extend the borders so they can be easily centered in the quilting hoop. This is easier than basting fabric to the quilt edge.

Binding and Other Edge Variations

The choice of binding fabrics and designs is similar to selecting the appropriate necklace to finish an ensemble for a special occasion.

BINDINGS AS NECKLACES

The "necklace" of a quilt might be a degree darker in value; see *Asilomar Circles I* (page 63). The necklace might be a degree lighter with subtle texture as in *Circles II* (page 64), *Japanese Circles II* (page 66), and *Vert Coterie* (page 5). The necklace might be a lively or high-contrast accent, see *Circles I* (page 13), *African Circles I* (page 8), and *African Circles II* (page 39).

Should you cut the binding on the grain or on the bias?

I normally cut 2¼"-wide strips on the crossgrain. Join the ends with diagonal seams to reduce bulk, and press the strip in half lengthwise with the right side of the fabric facing out. If the fabric pattern would be enhanced by cutting on the bias, that's what I do (see *African Circles I* on page 8).

CORDING VARIATION

A binding variation that works well for *Circle Play* quilts is the implied roundness of cording for the quilt edge finish. In *Japanese Circles I* (page 31) the black cording between the quilt top and the beige/brown necklace of the bias binding repeats the black lattice of the featured circles.

Consider making your own cording. You can choose the size of the cording to use, and covering your own allows more fabric and pattern choices. Wash to preshrink your cording, in a mesh lingerie bag, to avoid shrinkage problems later.

Cut the fabric for the cording on the bias. Roll a tape measure around the cording to determine the width of the fabric strips to cut. It is easier to sew the fabric around the cording if the strips are cut slightly wider than needed. Trim the excess seam allowance after sewing. Join the ends on the diagonal.

Tape the ends of the cording to prevent unraveling during handling. Use a cording or zipper foot to sew the fabric around the cord. It is helpful to use a sewing machine that has a needle position adjustment. Stitch with the cut edges and wrong sides of the fabric together, with the cord inside, stitching gently against the cord. A second or third stitching against the cording will tighten it further.

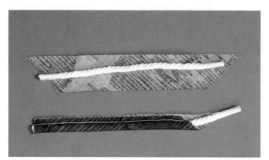

Cut the strip wider than the cording and trim after sewing.

Align the raw edges of the cording strip and the quilt front. Sew the cording to the quilt

Use your needle position control to move the needle to the left when you sew the cording to the quilt, stitching close to the cording. When you reach a corner, stop ¼" from the cut edge with the needle in the down position (in the fabric). Lift the presser foot and clip the seam allowance of the cording to the needle, but not through the stitching line. Rotate the quilt and align the cording seam allowance on the quilt edge to form a right angle; continue stitching to the next corner. I use a stiletto, the point of a seam ripper, or a long porcupine quill to gently ease the cording into the right angle during stitching.

To prevent bulkiness when adding binding to a corded seam start on the opposite side from where the cording was joined. Turn the binding to the back and hand stitch.

Align the raw edges of the binding with the edge of the quilt. Stitch the binding close to the cording, on the outside of the cording.

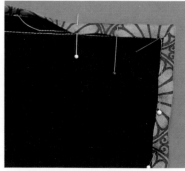

Turn the binding to the back and pin it in place. Hand-stitch the binding to the back of the quilt.

Facing the Edges

For some *Circle Play* quilts a soft-finished edge such as that used on *Obi Circles I* (page 50) is all that is needed. This technique is similar to a garment facing with one exception: the corner bulk. Fabric strips for facings are cut 2½" wide by the length needed for each side of the quilt. To keep the bulk in the corners to a minimum cut four 4½" x 4½" squares and stitch a binding strip to each of two corners. Trim the inside corner in a curve to meet the long strips.

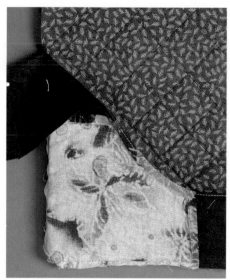

Sew a square to the corner. Sew a binding strip to each side of the square. Trim the corner into a currve. Press the seams open and turn under the edge and sew.

Finish the inside edge of the facing corners and strips by turning ¼" to the wrong side and stitching along the fold as shown. Pin the four prepared facings to the edge of the quilt back. Align the corners and leave the excess ends of the facing strips to meet along each of the four sides. These ends can be joined in overlapped seams as shown below, or joined with a straight seam (rather than a diagonal one).

Join the ends of the facings.

Stitch the pinned facings to the quilt, shortening the machine stitch length for ½" at each side of the corners to reinforce them.

Add a second line of stitching to sew the seam allowances to the facings so the facings don't show on the front of the quilt; this is called "understitching" in dressmaking.

Understitch the seam allowances to the facing.

Begin understitching close to the corner and finish stitching close to the next corner. You will not be able to understitch right up to the corner. The facing will roll to the back of the quilt; hand stitch to the back as you would a binding. To turn a smooth corner do not trim the bulk.

Place your index finger in the corner. Fold the seam allowances firmly the way you want them to lay inside the facing. Pinch the folded seam allowances with your thumb on the outside against your finger (on the inside) and turn the whole corner right-side out. It should be square. Rather than trimming off the seam allowances (the "garbage") you have "organized the garbage." I learned this technique and phrase, along with most of my sewing techniques, from my friend and teaching partner, Mabel Huseby.

Cording and Facings

Facings can be combined with cording for a softer finish than binding but with more pizzazz than the subtlety of a facing alone (see *Plaid Circles I* on page 54).

The back corner of a quilt with a corded edge and a fitted facing

The front corner of a quilt with a corded edge and a fitted facing

I recommend adding a hanging sleeve at both the top and bottom of the quilt, so it hangs smoothly. Sign the quilt front using a permanent pen, and add a label on the back with your name, address, telephone number, the name and size of the quilt, date completed, and anything else that seems important. I write directly on the quilt because it discourages theft; this is more permanent than a label.

With the design issues and construction steps complete for Circle Play I quilts, let's go back to the remaining fabrics we gathered in Chapter 1, and those fabrics that were irresistible and had to be added, and turn to the final design chapter: Going Beyond Circle Play I.

COSMIC RIBBONS, 83½" x 93½", designed by Gudny Campbell, made by the Monterey Peninsula Quilters Guild, machine quilted by Kathy Sandbach.

Going Beyond Circle Play I is a second or third (or more) opportunity to work/play with the next generation of the previous quilt. Place the set of circles you reserved in Chapter 3 on the design wall (page 24).

The circles are beautiful in a different way than *Plaid Circles I* (page 54). These circles come from the background of the appliquéd circles in the previous quilt, so they have a lovely value flow and "belong" together. The second-generation quilt may have a very different feel than the original if you exchange calm support fabrics for the busy fabrics in the first quilt, as in *African Circles II* on page 39. One of the most obvious characteristics of this new set of circles is that the half- and quarter-division seams are not equal parts. This literally keeps them off center in the blocks, and encourages them to dance and give excitement to the next quilts.

Try various arrangements on your design wall to explore possibilities such as value flows from center outward, from a corner inward, or from top to bottom. In Margaret Miller's book, *Blockbuster Quilts*, there is an excellent discussion of this topic.

Try new quilt shapes: square, rectangle, or kimono shape. Remember there are no rules that you must use all of the new set of circles, or that you cannot make more whole or pieced circles. Notice that color, as well as the number of blocks, subtly changes in Diana Johnston's five quilts on pages 70–71.

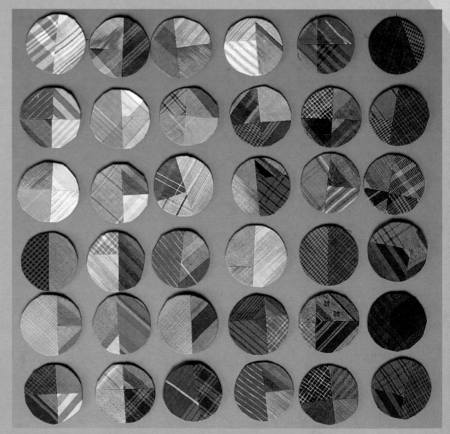

Second-generation 2" circles cut from the background of the appliquéd circles in *Plaid Circles I* (page 54)

Try arranging all the circles with the dominant seamlines on the diagonal. Then try the dominant seamlines in an on-point setting.

Study your collection of support fabrics. Perhaps you have added more fabrics of one color or have special textures you weren't able to include in the first quilt. Arrange the support fabrics by value flow—light to dark—to see if the second generation quilt might have a different feeling, one of dark mystery or airy and light.

MOONLIGHT, 28" x 28", by Tomoko Yoshihashi. A second-generation circle on the lower edge creates a wonderful and unexpected transparency with the triangles above it, creating a very effective border treatment.

You don't need to work with the full set of circles, especially if you have used some in the previous quilt. Tomoko Yoshihashi successfully used second-generation circles to break up the inner border on her quilt, *Moonlight*, by covering the inner border on three sides. The fourth border appears to have a circle behind it. The circles can continue the color flow, or create a transparent effect by the careful placement of the circle fabrics.

A guideline for using a next generation of circles is to repeat the same divisions in the background block as is in the pieced circle. For example, place a three-part circle onto a background block made of three triangles. One exception is a circle from a mitered corner. The mitered portion of the circle works best with a half-square triangle for value- and line-flow. The mitered circle portion could also be placed onto a mitered striped block.

Asilomar Circles I also makes use of several second-generation circles. These circles can serve a variety of functions. A second circle can cover a boring or plain circle, and make it more interesting as shown in the photo below.

A second circle can be used to *expose* a special texture used in the block that has been covered by the first circle.

The third function of a second circle is to repeat a design portion of another circle in the quilt. By setting the second circle at the edge of the lighter lavender circle, a crescent is formed that repeats the crescent of the silk circle two blocks to its left.

Details from **ASILOMAR CIRCLES I**

Finally, notice that the overlaying circle does not need to come from the corresponding block beneath it. In the photo below, the second circle is used *artistically* to emphasize the radial design of the beige silk beneath, and *functionally* to cover the tiny moth holes in the beige silk.

Even after using 4 circles (trimmed from behind the first quilt) on the surface of the same quilt, there are still 32 circles to use in a second-generation quilt! You can create new circles from the leftover triangles of the first quilt. Your imagination and life span are the only limits!

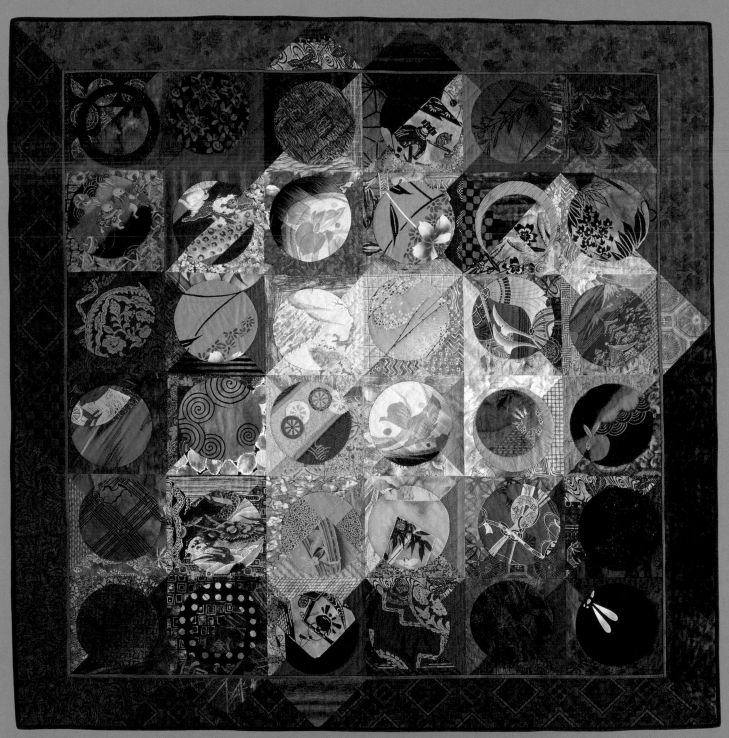

ASILOMAR CIRCLES I, 62" x 62", by Reynola Pakusich,

Use a set of second-generation circles to challenge yourself to explore various value flows of light and dark. In *Circles II* the background color was matched to each circle but the value was slightly darker.

CIRCLES II, 45" x 45", by Reynola Pakusich.

The texture change between the two fabrics creates interest, while the value change makes the circles appear as holes in the swaths of light and dark.

CIRCLES III, 30" x 30" by Reynola Pakusich.

In *Circles III* (the circles were trimmed from behind *Circles II*), the value change was reversed, keeping the background triangle a degree lighter than the circle. This results in a transparent effect between the circles and the background flow.

African Circles II and *III* demonstrate textural, rather than value, challenges. Because the background triangles chosen for *African Circles I* (page 8) were of little textural interest, the resulting *African Circles II* (page 39) circles were quite plain. By continuing to use mostly tone-on-tone fabrics with little contrast in color or value, the subsequent quilt has a more folk-art than an ethnic-African appearance. The folk-art jungle border adds to the character of the quilt.

African Circles III returns to a more authentic African appearance. At the same time, the impact of the pieced circles is reduced by using more graphic African fabrics for the triangles.

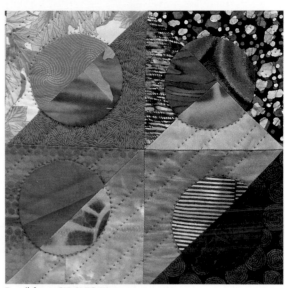

Detail from **CIRCLES III**

AFRICAN CIRCLES III, 40" x 40", by Reynola Pakusich.

JAPANESE CIRCLES II,
45½" x 45½",
by Reynola Pakusich.

Japanese Circles II uses all of the circles cut from *Japanese Circles I* (page 31) to create rings, or doughnuts, that expose some of the beautiful fabrics covered by the circles and add interest to the area that is a swath of light.

You can create more visual interest by letting parts of the rings nearly disappear while others have higher contrast. This soft or hard edge can be accomplished by changing or repeating the two textures and the degree of value contrast.

Construction of the rings or doughnuts is easy. The circles are made the same way as described in Chapter 2, then appliquéd onto the previous circle and trimmed from behind. Quilting in the center of the donut helps "push" the center area back and visually enhances the ring.

Study the series quilts by Diana Johnston on pages 70–71 to see the creative way she uses successive generations of circles. The subsequent generations are beautiful because the first quilt was. They are just different than the previous one.

I hope you enjoy your *Circle Play* experience with as much as I do. I conclude with the words of warning my husband gives my new quilter friends: It can be addicting!

JUPITER'S MOONS, 42" x 42", by Ionne McCauley. The hand-dyed background fabric emphasizes the title mood. Circles integrate beautifully with the blocks for this unusual setting.

WEARABLE ART JACKET II,
by Mary Margarite Eighme.
Smaller circles using a higher
contrasting print creates
dramatic wearable art.

ROCKS IN MY POND, 40" x 40", by Teri Bever. This is a creative variation of circles; Teri used a variety of ovals, cleverly playing off both design lines of the fabric and seamlines. The oval placement suggests graceful motion in a koi pond.

OBI II, 29" x 49", by Reynola Pakusich. Beading by Susan Wells Hall. The Japanese feel of this second-generation quilt is continued by the repetition of the *Obi I* silk used in several of the background triangles and the addition of a silk brocade border fabric from a vintage kimono. The quilting in the border follows the design of the woven silk fabric.

1

AT DT'S RETREAT, 54" x 54", by Diana Johnston. This exciting collection of fabrics for Diana's first quilt includes fabrics given to her at a retreat with her quilting friends.

Generations of Circles

Diana Johnston used the fabric cut from behind the circles of the earlier quilts to make the circles for the next quilts in this series of 6 quilts, 5 of which are shown here.

Notice that the later quilts in the series are smaller in size and the circles are smaller, too. The sixth and final quilt is only 8½" square.

2

HOME ALONE, 47" x 47", by Diana Johnston. Working alone on this second-generation quilt resulted in more greens. Notice two fabrics were effectively used for the inner fold between the design field and the border.

3 CITRUS SLICES, 38" x 38", by Diana Johnston. This third-generation quilt results in strong "slices" of color.

5 CINCO DE OH MY!, 16" x 16", by Diana Johnston. The fifth of this series demonstrates more variations of the value-flow integrated with the pieced circles. The use of circle-theme fabrics also highlights the circles.

6 NO SIXTH SENSE, 8½" x 8½", by Diana Johnston. In this miniature sixth quilt the quilting lines were used to create both the texture and to stitch down the fused tiny circles. The result is a successful culmination of the series.

FIRST GENERATION BRIGHTS,
59" x 59", by Cory Volkert. The use of mitered stripes in the center creates a subtle focal point that is repeated in the outer shadows of dark and light values. This quiltmaker skillfully arranged a wide variety of fabrics for the circles.

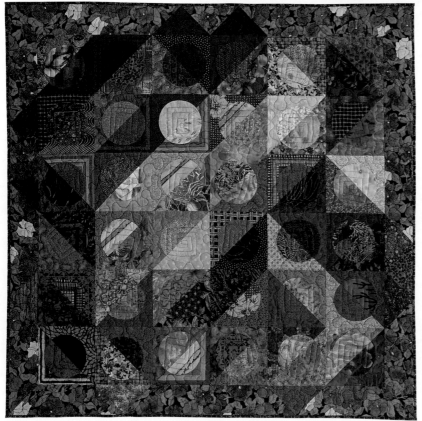

SECOND GENERATION BRIGHTS,
49" x 49", by Cory Volkert. The value-flows are subtler than the first-generation quilt while continuity is achieved through using the circle fabric from First Generation Brights for the border fabric of this quilt.

AMATEUR DECORATING, 43" x 43", by Michelle Moore. The use of geometric textures with the florals of the decorator fabric creates a wonderful overall balance. Notice how well the lines of the circles are integrated with the design lines of the background blocks. From the collection of Denise Gonsalves.

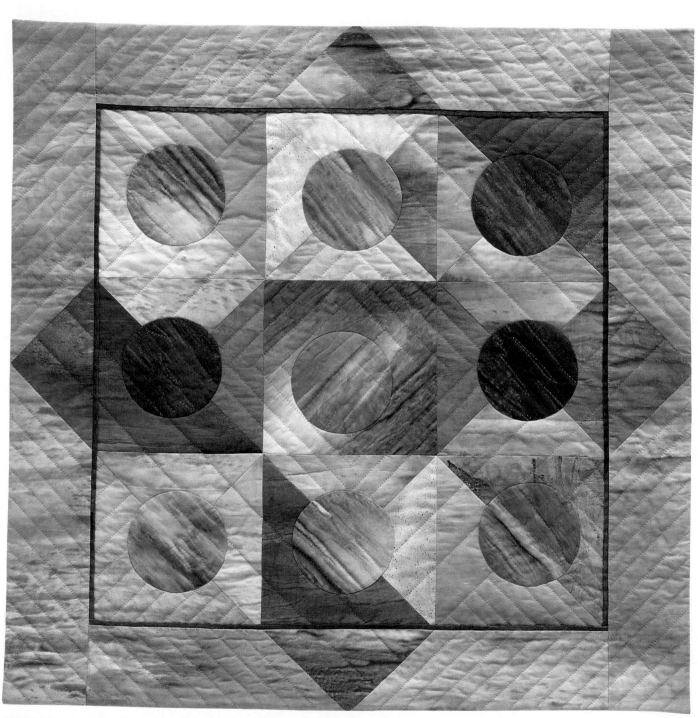

PLANETARY NOTIONS, 27" x 27", by Kristin Thompson. The use of a single run of Sky Dyes fabrics (see Resources, page 79) creates layers of tranquility.

GHOSTLY MOONS, 45" x 45", by Ionne McCauley. In this creative nine-patch format the pieced circles from *Jupiter's Moons* (page 67) form wonderful transparencies.

Glossary of Terms

CENTER FIELD: The middle area of the quilt; the focal point and background, excluding borders.

CUT SIZE: See **Finished vs. cut size.**

DESIGN LINE/DESIGN-LINE FLOW: Lines that follow the shapes printed on fabrics that can appear to continue from one fabric to another without interruption by a seamline.

FINISHED VS. CUT SIZE: The size of a triangle with the ¼" seam allowances included is the cut size; the size of the triangle after the edges are stitched to another fabric using a ¼" seam allowance is the finished size.

FLOATING: A visual effect in which the focus image is surrounded by the background rather than having a border or outline touching it.

HARD EDGE: Refers to a high degree of value contrast between two fabrics; usually between the circle or portion of it and the background square or triangular portion of the square (for comparison see **Soft edge**).

ROUGH-CUT: Cutting around a template or shape leaving a generous seam allowance; the resulting piece will later be shaped accurately with a circle template of freezer paper.

SASHIKO: Early eighteenth century Japanese wives made warm clothes by stitching two pieces of heavy fabric together using fine decorative stitches throughout the entire garment. Patterns were adopted from kimono prints, fabric weaves, and nature such as, bamboo, ocean waves, flowers, etc.

SEAMLINE: The line of stitching that joins two pieces of fabric; a visual opportunity for value and color contrast.

SMOOTHING: To lower the degree of texture or value contrast between fabrics.

SOFT EDGE: A low degree of value contrast between two fabrics that causes the viewer to search for the seamline (edge) between those fabrics (for comparison see **Hard edge**).

TEXTURE: There are two types: visual texture refers to the pattern printed on or woven into the fabric, such as stripes, flowers, painterly strokes, and so on. Tactile texture refers to the physical feel of the fabric, such as silky satin, corduroy wales, etched velvet; brocade and damask have both visual and tactile texture; the *Circle Play* concept primarily manipulates visual texture.

TRUE-UP: Checking and trimming the blocks so they are the same size before going on to the next construction unit; blocks are trued-up before they are sewn together.

VALUE/ VALUE FLOW: How the lightness or darkness of a fabric can appear to continue from one piece to another without interruption by a seamline.

WELT: A double layer of fabric that has only one side stitched into the seam; the folded side may then be pressed in either direction from the seam; used primarily for the visual effect of color and design.

TEACHING SAMPLE: An in-process quilt top that is used to demonstrate a process or effect usually shown in several stages or steps.

ZONE: An area of the quilt that has similar texture or value, such as putting all the busy fabrics next to each other or all the bright fabrics in the same zone; zoning is a way to organize disparate textures, colors, or values.

About the Author

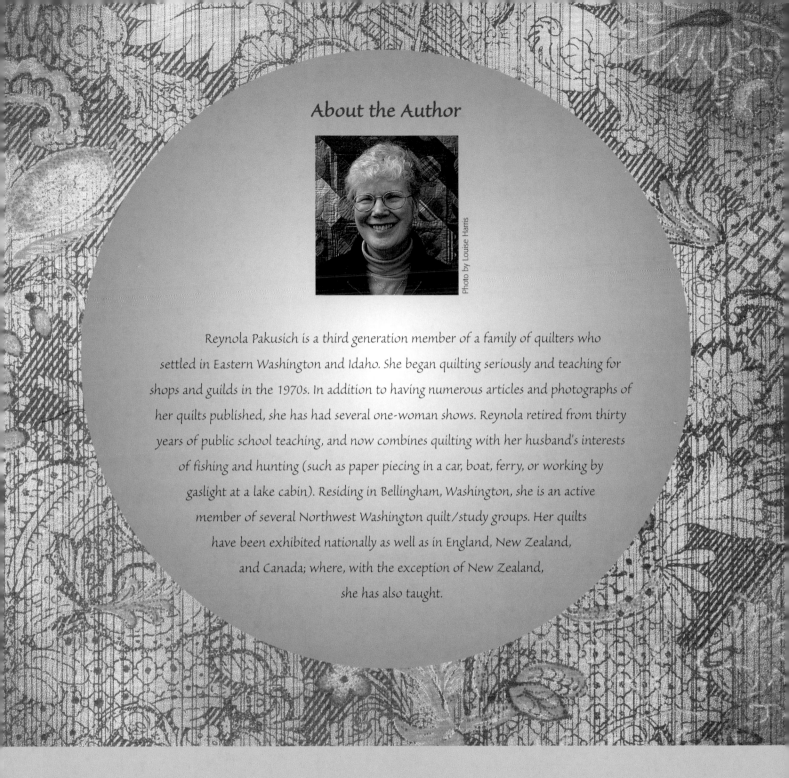

Photo by Louise Harris

Reynola Pakusich is a third generation member of a family of quilters who settled in Eastern Washington and Idaho. She began quilting seriously and teaching for shops and guilds in the 1970s. In addition to having numerous articles and photographs of her quilts published, she has had several one-woman shows. Reynola retired from thirty years of public school teaching, and now combines quilting with her husband's interests of fishing and hunting (such as paper piecing in a car, boat, ferry, or working by gaslight at a lake cabin). Residing in Bellingham, Washington, she is an active member of several Northwest Washington quilt/study groups. Her quilts have been exhibited nationally as well as in England, New Zealand, and Canada; where, with the exception of New Zealand, she has also taught.

Bibliography

Horton, Roberta, *The Fabric Makes the Quilt*, C&T Publishing, Lafayette, California, 1995.

Miller, Margaret J., *Blockbuster Quilts*, That Patchwork Place, Bothel, Washington, 1991. Out-of-print; locate in your guild library or used bookstores.

Wolfrom, Joen, *The Magical Effects of Color*, C&T Publishing, Lafayette, California, 1992.

WHY NOT BLACK AND WHITE?
21" x 26", by Maggie Weyers.
Skillful use of the black and white
prints allows some circle edges to
fade, encouraging the viewer to
look further.

LEAVES OF SAPPHIRE, 45" x 45",
by Teri Bever. The color, value, and
clarity of the solids lend an Amish
feel to this quilt. The lines of the
print's leaves work off the block
seamlines and are assisted by the
appliquéd over-leaves.

Resources
EQUIPMENT AND SUPPLIES

Fabric Sources

BIZARRE BAZAAR
Hard-to-find ethnic fabrics from around the world.
P.O. Box 356, Indianola, WA 98342
Tel: 360-297-4541 Fax: 360-297-4506
Email: smilling@silverlink.net

FL AIR FABRIC DESIGN
Hand-designed airbrushed cotton and/or silkfabrics in
textures and colors as well as small images that are useful for both
circle and support fabrics.
550 North Hawk Ridge Place, Camano Island, WA 98292
Tel: 888-617-3677 Fax: 360-424-8064
Website: www.flairdesigns.com
Email: flair@camano.net

JUST IMAGINATION
Many national quilters think this is the best hand-dyer of cotton
fabrics currently available.
P.O. Box 583, Burlington, WA 98233
Tel: 360-755-1611
Website: www.justimagination.com

KARMA PLACE
Vintage kimonos and obis in silk, wool, and cotton at
reasonable prices; occasionally has obi remnants available; special-
izes in antique Japanese furniture.
3533 Chuckanut Drive, Bow, WA 98232
Tel: 360-766-6716
Email: deymian@karmaplace.com

KIMONO KREATIONS
Whole and pieces of vintage kimonos for sale; especially wonderful
woolens.
215 Islander Way, Anacortes, WA 98221
Tel: 360-293-1031

SKY DYES
Hand-painted and dyed fabrics.
Mickey Lawler
P.O. Box 370116, West Hartford, CT 06137
Tel: 860-232-1429 Fax: 860-236-9117
Email: skydyes@aol.com
Website: www.skydyes.com

Index

Other Fine books from C&T Publishing

All About Quilting from A to Z, From the Editors and Contributors of Quilter's Newsletter Magazine and Quiltmaker Magazine

America from the Heart: Quilters Remember September 11, 2001, Karey Bresenhan

Art of Classic Quiltmaking, The, Harriet Hargrave & Sharyn Craig

Art of Machine Piecing, The: How to Achieve Quality Workmanship Through a Colorful Journey, Sally Collins

Color Play: Easy Steps to Imaginative Color in Quilts, Joen Wolfrom

Contemporary Classics in Plaids & Stripes: 9 Projects from Piece 'O Cake Designs, Linda Jenkins & Becky Goldsmith

Curves in Motion: Quilt Designs & Techniques, Judy Dales

Fast, Fun & Easy Fabric Bowls: 5 Reversible Shapes to Use & Display, Linda Johanson

Heirloom Machine Quilting, 3rd Edition: Comprehensive Guide to Hand-Quilting Effects Using Your Sewing Machine, Harriet Hargrave

Mastering Machine Appliqué, 2nd Edition: The Complete Guide Including: • Invisible Machine Appliqué • Satin Stitch • Blanket Stitch & Much More, Harriet Hargrave

Piecing: Expanding the Basics, Ruth B. McDowell

Quilts from the Civil War: Nine Projects, Historic Notes, Diary Entries, Barbara Brackman

Radiant New York Beauties: 14 Paper-Pieced Quilt Projects, Valori Wells

Show Me How to Machine Quilt: A Fun, No-Mark Approach, Kathy Sandbach

Simple Fabric Folding for Christmas: 14 Festive Quilts & Projects, Liz Aneloski

Skydyes: A Visual Guide to Fabric Painting, Mickey Lawler

Smashing Sets: Exciting Ways to Arrange Quilt Blocks, Margaret J. Miller

Start Quilting with Alex Anderson, 2nd Edition: Six Projects for First-Time Quilters, Alex Anderson

Strips 'n Curves: A New Spin on Strip Piecing, Louisa L. Smith

Visual Dance, The: Creating Spectacular Quilts, Joen Wolfrom

Workshop with Velda Newman, A: Adding Dimension to Your Quilts, Velda E. Newman

FRUIT SALAD, 36" x 36", by Patricia Cotter. The clear colors of the fruit print give this a l940s look while still achieving a lovely value flow behind the circles.

For more information, ask for a free catalog:
C&T Publishing, Inc.
P.O. Box 1456
Lafayette, CA 94549
(800) 284-1114
Email: ctinfo@ctpub.com
Website: www.ctpub.com

For quilting supplies:
Cotton Patch Mail Order
3405 Hall Lane, Dept.CTB
Lafayette, CA 94549
(800) 835-4418
(925) 283-7883
Email: quiltusa@yahoo.com
Website: www.quiltusa.com

Note: Fabrics used in the quilts shown may not be currently available because fabric manufacturers keep most fabrics in print for only a short time.